Abortion

5/02

Abortion

by Allison Lassieur

Lucent
Books

LUCENT *Overview Series*

Library of Congress Cataloging-in-Publication Data

Lassieur, Allison.
    Abortion / by Allison Lassieur.
        p.   cm. — (Lucent overview series)
    Includes bibliographical references and index.
    Summary: Discusses abortion and related issues including clinic
violence and its effect, parental notification, consent, and privacy
issues, partial birth abortion, the safety and privacy of RU 486 and
medical abortions.
    ISBN 1-56006-818-3 (hardcover : alk. paper)
    1. Abortion—Juvenile literature. [1. Abortion.] I. Title. II. Series.
RG734 .L37   2001
363.46—dc21
                                                        00-009250

Copyright © 2001 by Lucent Books, Inc.
P.O. Box 289011, San Diego, CA 92198-9011
Printed in the U.S.A.

Contents

Introduction

ABORTION HAS BECOME one of the most controversial issues of our time. Politicians argue over the legal aspects of abortion. Religious and pro-life groups work to make their views and beliefs about abortion known. Pro-choice organizations work just as hard to speak out for their views. Some people choose to try to change laws or create new legislation that will reflect their positions on abortion. Others choose to block access to clinics and resort to violence to make sure their voices are heard.

Almost no one remains untouched by the abortion controversy. Patients and clinic workers are sometimes prevented from entering medical facilities because of blockades and threats of violence. Ordinary people are exposed to television commercials, billboards, and other forms of media that promote antiabortion and pro-choice beliefs.

Although there have been a few attempts to find common ground, both sides of the debate find little to agree on. This is due mainly to vast differences between the basic beliefs and values of each side. The antiabortion side is committed to respecting an individual's right to life, even if that individual is not yet born. They believe that the weak and helpless should be protected at all costs and allowed to develop to their full potential. Most antiabortion advocates are also deeply religious, and their moral convictions coupled with their religious beliefs demand that they actively work to make sure those beliefs prevail. They believe that what they view as the sanctity of life gives them the responsibility to uphold their convictions even at personal cost.

On the other side, pro-choice advocates stress freedom of the individual. They advocate the idea that women have the right to determine their destinies by controlling when and how they bear children. They believe decisions of morality and personal choice should be made only by those who will be affected by those decisions, and that government should not interfere in personal choices.

The question of abortion is so contentious because it pits these two positions against one another in a way that is impossible to compromise. Pro-choice groups focus on the rights of women and downplay the status and rights of unborn children. Antiabortion advocates, on the other hand, prefer to elevate the rights of the unborn above those of the woman in many cases.

The Supreme Court entered the debate in 1973 with what is possibly its most influential—and hotly contested—ruling of the twentieth century, *Roe v. Wade*. In that ruling, the Court legalized abortion in the first three months of pregnancy and established certain parameters for states to restrict abortion later in pregnancy. Instead of

Pro-choice advocates believe that women should make their own choices regarding reproduction and that the government should not interfere.

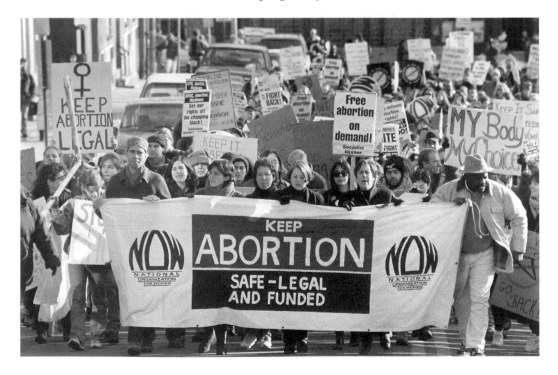

settling the abortion question, however, the ruling only fueled the controversy. Today abortion is still one of the most divisive issues in the country.

Over the years, specific aspects of the debate have emerged as some of the most important and controversial issues facing Americans. The most shocking development has been that of clinic violence. Organizations such as Operation Rescue have led the efforts to blockade clinics and deny women access to abortion services. The violence escalated until, in the 1990s, gunmen murdered a number of abortion providers in shootings that stunned the nation. These killings revealed how far the violence had been allowed to go, and resulted in legislation that eventually curbed most of the violence and reestablished some peace in communities that had been torn apart.

Minor's rights and partial-birth abortions

The question of whether minors had a right to seek abortions without parental notification or consent became a hot issue in the 1990s. *Roe v. Wade* stated that minors had this right, but in the years since, states—with the backing of powerful antiabortion groups—passed restrictive notification and consent laws. Pro-choice advocates have insisted that young women have the same rights to seek abortions privately as do adults, but the courts continued to disagree. This question affects thousands of young women every year, and although most states now have consent or notification laws on the books, the debate is still alive.

Perhaps the most controversial and talked-about issue in the abortion debate is the late-term abortion procedure known as "partial-birth" abortion. In the mid-1990s, antiabortion organizations began drawing attention to this relatively rarely used medical procedure and proceeded to make it a huge political issue. For years, these groups worked to ban the procedure, and pro-choice advocates battled against them just as fiercely. Finally, in 2000, the Supreme Court ruled that existing bans were unconstitutional, but the decision left room for other legislation to be passed that could prohibit the procedure.

Finally, one facet of the abortion controversy that is poised to change the entire scope of the debate is RU 486 and medical abortion. When the drug RU 486 was developed in the 1980s, it was heralded as a breakthrough in abortion research. Women would be able to take medication to end a pregnancy, and they could have an abortion in the privacy of a doctor's office or even in their own homes. No longer would they have to face a screaming group of antiabortion protesters in front of a clinic. Physicians would no longer fear assassination, for protesters would not know that they were prescribing the drug. However, it was not that simple. Antiabortion protests, government bans, marketing delays, and the lingering controversy over abortion kept the drug out of the United States for years. Even after the drug was approved in the United States, questions remained.

Antiabortion advocates believe that every individual has a right to life, even those not yet born.

These topics are the ones that remain unresolved in the ongoing abortion controversy, and it is unlikely that any of them will be settled in the near future. Until they are, the debate will continue to rage.

1

What Is Abortion?

IF YOU ASK a number of people to define abortion the chances are good that there will be a different answer each time. To some, abortion is murder. These people believe that life begins at the moment of conception and therefore abortion is wrong in any circumstance. Others believe that abortion is a question of personal privacy. They think that a woman has the right to decide for herself whether to have a child and that her right to control her own destiny supersedes any rights as a person that the embryo or fetus might have. A few of these people believe that there should be no restrictions at all on a woman's right to choose a safe, legal abortion.

Surveys have shown, however, that most people find themselves somewhere in the middle of the debate. While most people believe that a woman should have the right to have an abortion early in a pregnancy, they also seem to think that it is reasonable for some restrictions to be placed on late-term abortions.

A complication in the abortion debate has arisen in the past few years, and this is the question of what, exactly, constitutes an abortion. Is abortion merely the surgical removal of a fetus? Is birth control that prevents conception a form of abortion? Are birth control methods that prevent a fertilized egg from embedding itself in the uterus, such as IUDs, actually abortion methods? More recently, with the development of drugs that can either expel a fetus from the uterus or prevent the fertilized egg from attaching, the answers have grown even more vague. If a woman takes a pill to prevent a pregnancy before she knows whether she is pregnant, is that abortion?

For years, people have disagreed on the questions of what abortion is and what constitutes an abortion. The standard definition of an abortion, according to the National Abortion Federation, is the following: "Abortion is the removal of a fetus from the uterus before it is mature enough to live on its own. When this happens spontaneously, it is called a miscarriage. Induced abortion is brought about deliberately by a medical procedure that ends pregnancy."[1]

Approximately 88 percent of all induced abortions are performed during the first trimester, which is the first three months of pregnancy. More than half are performed within the first two months of pregnancy. Currently, there are two forms of induced abortion. One is called surgical abortion. This method ends a pregnancy by emptying the uterus (or womb) with special medical instruments. The other form of abortion is medical abortion. This is caused by taking specific medications that will end pregnancy.

A fetus in the first trimester of pregnancy, when most abortions are performed.

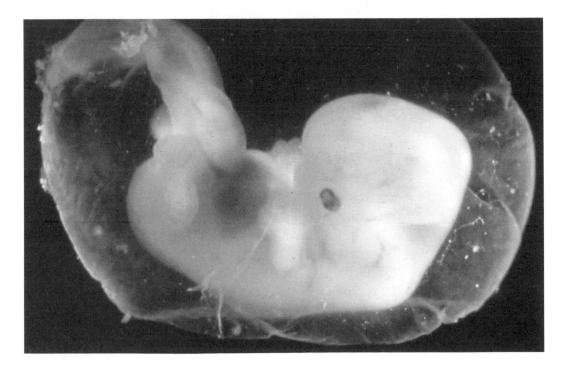

Before either method is used, it must be determined that a woman is indeed pregnant. The medical professional who is caring for the patient must also determine how far along the pregnancy is. Most health professionals usually measure a pregnancy in terms of how much time has passed since the patient's last menstrual period. The patient is given a pregnancy test and a physical examination. Some health-care workers also provide an ultrasound test, which uses sound waves to view the inside of the uterus. In most circumstances, medical abortions can be safely performed prior to seven weeks after the woman's last menstrual period. Surgical abortions are performed between six and twelve weeks.

Surgical abortion

There are three types of surgical abortion. If less than thirteen to fifteen weeks have passed since the patient's last menstrual period, she is considered to be in her first trimester. The most common abortion procedure during this time frame is called vacuum aspiration, or suction curettage. In this method, the health-care worker opens the cervix (the entrance to the uterus) and removes the contents of the uterus, which includes the fetus and the placenta.

This procedure is most commonly done in outpatient clinics and doctors' offices. The health-care worker inserts an instrument into the patient's vagina that will gently open, or dilate, the walls of the cervix. Once the cervix is dilated, the health-care worker inserts a small tube, called a cannula, which is connected to an aspirator machine. This machine is similar to the machines that dentists use to clear the mouth of saliva. The mild suction of the machine removes the contents of the uterus.

Suction curettage takes about five or ten minutes. Although the procedure is quick, some patients do experience pain, cramping, and some bleeding that is similar to menstrual bleeding. After a brief recovery time of a few minutes to an hour, the patient is allowed to go home.

The second method of surgical abortion is known as dilation and evacuation. This procedure is somewhat more

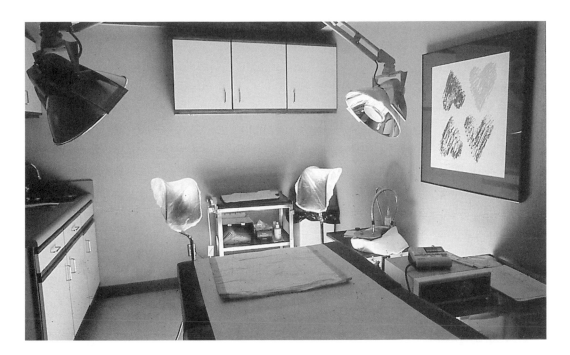

complicated because it is generally performed during the second trimester of the pregnancy. During this time, the fetus is larger and there is a greater blood supply to the uterus. Only about one-tenth of the abortions in the United States are performed between thirteen and twenty weeks, so this procedure is not as common.

Two of the three types of surgical abortion do not require hospitalization and may be done in outpatient clinics such as this one is Des Moines, Iowa.

The dilation and evacuation method of abortion is very similar to the suction curettage method. This procedure is mainly done in outpatient clinics but is occasionally performed in hospitals. The health-care worker dilates the patient's cervix, but it may take longer to open it to a width that is safe. The health-care worker then uses suction to remove the contents of the uterus. Once the suction is complete, the health-care worker uses another instrument, called a curette, to examine the uterus and determine that there is no more fetal tissue inside. If there is any tissue left, the worker gently scrapes it out with the curette. The entire procedure takes somewhat longer than the vacuum aspiration method, up to thirty minutes, and patients experience a greater amount of pain. Usually, pain medication is given to the patient before the procedure begins.

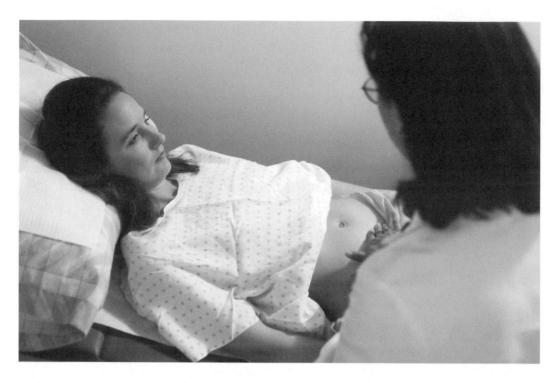

Health-care workers must accurately determine how advanced a pregnancy is before any abortion procedure.

Physicians and health-care workers recognize the increased risk of this procedure. Dr. Alan F. Guttmacher, founder of the Guttmacher Institute, cautioned physicians about this method:

> There is a clear consensus that safety in the performance of D&E depends on the accurate determination of the size of the fetus by ultrasound examination. The most serious error is to undertake the abortion of a patient in the second trimester through an inadequately dilated cervix or with inadequate instrumentation.[2]

The final method of surgical abortion is called induction. This procedure is performed during the later stages of pregnancy and is almost always done in a hospital by a physician. Less than two percent of all abortions are performed using this method. In the induction method, the patient is usually given anesthetic. Then the physician inserts a needle through the patient's abdomen and into the uterus and injects a solution of saline and medication. This induces, or begins, labor pains. A few hours later the patient goes into labor and expels the fetus.

Because this procedure is more complex, there is a higher risk of complications involved. Guttmacher explains,

> Because of the discomforts of this form of abortion, abortion by this technique has been limited to the care of hospitalized patients. . . . Abortion by this technique ordinarily requires a hospitalization of at least two days and, in the presence of complications, it can be substantially longer than that.[3]

Complications from surgical abortions

Studies suggest that having an abortion is actually safer than carrying a pregnancy to term. Each has its risks, however. Although complications from abortions are rare, they do occur.

In some cases, clotted blood inside the uterus creates complications. Guttmacher commented:

> There is a curious syndrome in which clotted blood blocks the internal cervical opening and additional bleeding into the uterus causes severe uterine distension. This can be suspected when a patient who has had an abortion within the previous 18 hours returns for care complaining of very severe, cramping uterine pain with minimal bleeding. The syndrome can be rapidly alleviated by repeat evacuation to remove the obstructing blood clots and establish drainage.[4]

When blood clots occur, the health-care worker must perform another suction procedure. Infections are another complication from abortion. They occur for a number of reasons, but they can be easily treated if they are recognized early.

A more serious complication of a suction curettage is cervical punctures or tears. There is always a risk of this when foreign objects, such as instruments and vacuum tubes, are inserted into the cervix and uterus. Some of these injuries heal on their own. Others may require a return visit to the doctor and stitches.

Although there are risks involved with the procedure, as there are with any medical procedure, the general medical consensus is that suction curettage is the safest abortion method. Guttmacher agrees: "The incidence of uterine perforation is extraordinarily low. Probably in the hands of experienced operators it should be substantially less than 1 percent."[5]

In a few cases, the abortion for some reason is not complete. Perhaps the health-care worker missed some tissue during the final exam, for example. Incomplete abortions are accompanied by symptoms such as infection and fever. An incomplete abortion may require a second abortion.

Some women experience excessive bleeding after an abortion. This is caused when the now-empty uterus does not contract and return to its prepregnancy condition. When this occurs, the uterus continues to expel blood, which can be dangerous. Excessive bleeding is a potentially serious complication that must be addressed by a doctor immediately.

Very rarely, a patient dies from complications of a legal abortion. Statistically, there is one death for every 160,000 women who have legal abortions. These deaths are usually a result of such things as heart attacks, reactions to anesthesia, or uncontrollable bleeding. However, studies show that death from complications of pregnancy are ten times greater.

At present, surgical abortions constitute a majority of the abortions in the United States In the last few years, however, a new kind of abortion technique has been developed: medical abortion. Medical abortion, unlike surgical abortion, does not require instruments. Instead, the abortion is brought about by taking specific medications that will end a pregnancy.

Medical abortion

Although medical abortion has been known to the medical community for years, it has never been widely recognized or used until recently. Medical abortions are achieved with a combination of drugs taken on a specific schedule. The first medication causes the uterine lining to break down, expelling the fertilized egg if it has attached to the lining. If the egg has not yet attached the breakdown of the lining prevents it from doing so. The second medication causes the uterus to contract and empty.

In a medical abortion, it is vital to determine how long the patient has been pregnant. The medications do not work well later in pregnancy, so medical abortions are not an option after about the seventh week of pregnancy. How-

Medical abortion is an option for women who have not yet reached the seventh week of pregnancy.

ever, medical abortions can be performed as early as pregnancy can be confirmed.

There are two steps to a medical abortion, and patients take a specific drug at each step. During the first step, a patient can be given one of two drugs. One is called methotrexate. This drug has been used in the United States since 1953 for certain types of cancer. Since then, medical research discovered that the drug could also be used to end unplanned pregnancies. Although the medication was not originally used for abortion, physicians can prescribe it for that purpose. Methotrexate is usually given in the form of a shot, although some patients prefer to take it orally.

Another medication that can be used in the first stage of a medical abortion is called mifepristone, also known as RU 486. It is a newer drug that was developed specifically to induce abortion. Patients take mifepristone in the form of a pill. It works by blocking a hormone called progesterone, which is necessary to sustain a pregnancy. If the body does not have this hormone, it causes the lining of the uterus to break down.

After one of these two drugs is taken, the patient waits a few days and then begins the second step of the medical abortion. During this step, she takes a drug called misoprostol. Misoprostol comes in tablet form, and these tablets are taken either orally or placed inside the vagina. Once the drug is used, the uterus begins to contract and expel its contents, which ends the pregnancy.

Medical abortions take a bit longer than surgical abortions to complete. A National Abortion Federation fact sheet explains,

> Medical abortion can take anywhere from 3 days to 3–4 weeks, and requires two visits to the clinic or medical office. These return visits are very important since there is no other way to be sure that the abortion has been completed. . . . About 1 in 20 women who try medical abortion will need to have a surgical abortion because the medication does not work for her.[6]

During the first step of a medical abortion, the patient usually experiences vaginal bleeding similar to a period. During the second step, some health-care professionals prefer to monitor the patient after she has taken misoprostol to make sure that the drug works properly. In many instances, the patient stays at the clinic or office for several hours so she will expel the uterine contents under medical supervision. Other patients choose to complete the procedure at home.

One significant difference between surgical abortions and medical abortions is the side effects that the patient experiences. Though there are few side effects with surgical abortion, the side effects of a medical abortion can include cramping, headache, nausea, vomiting, diarrhea, and heavy bleeding. These side effects are caused by the drug misoprostol.

Women who choose a medical abortion also experience more bleeding than women who choose a surgical abortion. This bleeding is from the breakdown and expulsion of the uterine lining. The cramps and bleeding usually fade after most of the embryonic tissue has been passed, but bleeding sometimes lasts for many days afterward.

A few days after the second medication is taken, the patient returns to the health-care facility for a follow-up exam. During that exam, the health-care worker can determine if the abortion has been successful.

Complications from medical abortion

Unlike surgical abortion, a medical abortion does not require that a health-care worker insert instruments inside a patient's body. There is no risk of traumatic injury as a result of a medical abortion. The most common complication of medical abortion is the heavy bleeding that many women experience. Because of this, women who choose to complete their abortions at home are encouraged to stay near a telephone and to have transportation in case emergency treatment is needed.

Although both surgical and medical abortions are irreversible, it is harder for some women to realize that they cannot reverse a medical abortion after they take the first pills. This misunderstanding is compounded by the fact that there is a length of time, sometimes days, between taking the pills and experiencing the abortion. As a result, some believe that if they simply do not take the second round of medication, their pregnancies will continue.

However, the pregnancy is ended by the first medications. Anyone who does not complete the cycle of medications is at greater risk of complications. Patients who consider medical abortion are carefully counseled about this to make sure that they completely understand that they cannot change their minds after the medication begins. For patients who are unsure about their decision, medical abortion might not be the best option.

The safety of both medical and surgical abortion is part of the ongoing abortion controversy. People on each side of the debate arm themselves with facts and evidence to support their views. Each side claims that the other distorts or misrepresents the facts. Pro-choice activists point to numerous studies that show the safety of both types of abortions. Antiabortion activists point to the complication rates in the same studies to prove otherwise.

Antiabortion organizations have used the question of the safety of medical abortions as a focus for their campaign against it. They hope to persuade the general public that medical abortions endanger the lives of women. As of yet, however, no long-term studies support this position. Conversely, although most recent studies indicate that medical abortions are indeed safe and effective, some medical professionals insist that more testing should be done. Regardless of the facts, it is likely that the debate will continue for years to come.

2

Clinic Violence and Its Effect

THE MORNING OF December 30, 1994, was a normal day in Brookline, Massachusetts. The local offices of Planned Parenthood, a national organization that provides reproductive health services, including abortion, had opened on time. Employees were just beginning their workday. Shortly after 10 A.M., a man dressed in black came into the office and asked, "Is this Planned Parenthood?" When told that it was, he pulled out a rifle and opened fire.

The receptionist, Shannon Lowney, was killed. Three people sitting in the waiting room were wounded. Amid the chaos, the mysterious shooter disappeared through the door and was gone. About ten minutes later, he entered another office nearby. This office, Preterm Health Services clinic, also provided abortion services. According to a witness, "A man came in with a black duffel bag. He took out a rifle. He said, 'Is this Preterm?' The woman answering the phone said, 'yes,' and he dropped the duffel bag and opened fire."[7]

The man shot the woman, Leanne Nichols, at least five times. She later died at a hospital. Then the gunman turned and shot a woman standing at a copy machine nearby. A third victim, Richard Seron, was a security guard at the clinic. Seron shot and wounded the man before the man fled on foot, still firing.

City police, state police, FBI agents, and other investigators were soon on the scene. They found an abandoned duffel bag that contained rounds of unused ammunition.

They also found a handgun and a store receipt inside the bag. Those clues led police to a twenty-three-year-old Hampton, Rhode Island, man named John Salvi.

People on both sides of the abortion debate were shocked and outraged at the killings. However, Salvi, who was later convicted for the shootings, was not the first gunman to attack an abortion clinic or to shoot people who worked at such clinics. The shootings at Planned Parenthood and Preterm were the fifth such attack in 1993 and 1994, two of the most violent years ever for abortion clinics and providers in the United States.

The clinic violence that gripped the United States in the 1990s struck a new chord of fear and anger in the country. Until that time, most clinic violence was in the form of blockades, threats, and intimidation. Although physicians and clinic workers had been singled out by some protesters, none had been killed. Now, however, for the first time, physicians and clinic workers were the targets of deadly force. These attacks were the culmination of two decades

Emergency personnel remove receptionist Shannon Lowney's body from the Planned Parenthood in Brookline, Massachusetts, after a gunman opened fire with a rifle.

of clinic violence that had swept through the country since the *Roe v. Wade* decision in 1973.

Violence on the doorstep

Although antiabortion activists protested clinics in the 1970s, it was not until the 1980s that organized, widespread violence began in earnest. In 1980, Ronald Reagan was elected president. His staunch antiabortion position energized the antiabortion movement, and his administration's silence when clinics were blockaded and attacked seemed to give extremists permission to continue their acts. Authors James Risen and Judy Thomas write in their book *Wrath of Angels*,

> The 1980 presidential election not only put a "pro-lifer" in the White House but gave instant legitimacy to anti-abortion militancy. After Reagan's inauguration, reversing *Roe v. Wade* no longer seemed far-fetched, and that prospect briefly reenergized the entire movement.[8]

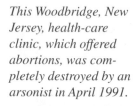

This Woodbridge, New Jersey, health-care clinic, which offered abortions, was completely destroyed by an arsonist in April 1991.

During Reagan's two terms in office, and through the administration of his successor George Bush, violence at health clinics that performed abortions rose dramatically around the country. In the 1980s and early 1990s, bomb-

ings, vandalism, blockades, and other forms of clinic violence were frequent occurrences at clinics. Death threats and other forms of intimidation increased. Many physicians and clinic workers around the country began wearing bulletproof vests to and from work. The atmosphere was tense and frightening.

This violence took many forms, but its purposes were the same: to shut down clinics and to make abortion a thing of the past. Today, more than a decade after Reagan left office, a majority of clinics still face the threat of violence every day.

What kinds of violence do clinics face?

One out of every five clinics in the United States experienced some kind of violence in 1999. Violence against clinics takes many forms. Some of the tactics of the antiabortion forces are not necessarily intended to harm anyone. Instead, many antiabortion activists openly admit, the intention of the unceasing intimidation is to wear down the resolve of the clinic employees. Antiabortion advocates believe that if they create an intimidating atmosphere, physicians and other health-care workers will abandon the clinics—one step away from closing them for good.

Harassment and vandalism

Day-to-day harassment of clinic workers comes mainly in the form of phone calls and letters. Antiabortion advocates might call a clinic and yell such things as "Baby killer!" or "You're going to hell" to whomever answers the phone. Clinics also routinely receive letters that threaten the clinic and those who work there. Sometimes, abortion foes pose as new patients just to get inside the clinic and harass employees. Gradually, clinic workers begin to dread answering telephone calls or talking to new patients for fear that the next one will come from the antiabortion movement.

Antiabortion advocates target the clinic buildings as well. More than one-third of clinics in the United States reported vandalism in 1999. This vandalism consists of spray painting graffiti; breaking windows; gluing doors shut; splattering paint; tampering with septic tanks, building ornaments, garbage dumpsters, and phone lines; strewing broken glass in clinic driveways; slashing tires; and even smearing human excrement on exterior walls.

This combination of harassment and vandalism can be devastating to those who work in abortion clinics. The constant strain of working under these conditions takes its toll. This harassment creates a sense of mistrust among the clinic workers, which ultimately undermines the job that they must perform every day. Many leave their jobs rather than endure the harassment.

Bombings

Since 1973, when the Supreme Court legalized abortion in the *Roe v. Wade* case, there have been hundreds of bombings and arsons at clinics around the country. In 1984 alone, more than twenty-five clinic arsons and bombings were reported. Until the 1990s, however, there had been no deaths from clinic bombings.

The potential for bombing deaths was always present, however, and in recent years, this threat attracted widespread attention. In 1997, a bomb rocked the Northside Family Planning Services center in Atlanta. Four people were inside the office, but no one was injured. An hour later, another bomb planted in a nearby garbage container exploded, injuring the police and bomb experts who had arrived at the scene. The second bomb had clearly been meant to injure any officials investigating the first bombing.

The first bombing in which a person died occurred a year later, on January 29, 1998, when a bomb exploded at a clinic in Birmingham, Alabama. This explosion killed a security officer and severely injured a nurse who worked at the clinic. A few months later, the nurse, Emily Lyons, testified before the House Judiciary Committee on Crime. She described her injuries that resulted from the bombing:

> I've spent almost thirty hours on an operating table in nine different operations, only to still have dozens of pieces of shrapnel permanently left in my body. I can't walk, drive a car, or go to work. . . . My left eye was destroyed and had to

be removed. My right eye was badly damaged. My right hand was mangled beyond repair. The skin was torn off my shins and my leg shattered. . . . My eardrum was ruptured and required extensive surgery. As a result, I am now a nurse who is unable to read, write, or stand for long periods of time. Instead of caring for others, others have to care for me.[9]

Although a majority of antiabortion organizations denounce clinic bombings, few have called for the violence to stop completely. A few have gone so far as to publicly support bombings as a way to prevent abortion.

Acid and disease attacks

In the last few years, clinics have faced new threats of acid and disease attacks. Butyric acid is a hazardous chemical that has been used in more than one hundred attacks since 1995. Although the chemical is not fatal, it causes severe nausea and other debilitating symptoms, and anyone exposed to it might need hospitalization. This chemical is so dangerous that it must be cleaned up by hazardous waste professionals, which creates enormous costs for both clinics and cities as well as forcing clinics to close, at least temporarily.

Another twist on the antiabortion threat emerged in the late 1990s. Clinics were threatened with attacks of anthrax, a contagious and potentially fatal disease. In 1999, thirty-nine clinics throughout the United States received anthrax threats. In the first two weeks of January 2000 alone, over thirty clinics in twenty-two states received such threats.

Internet threats

Other types of threats have been made possible with the emergence of Internet technology. Many individuals and organizations have created websites that promote their violent antiabortion ideology. Some sites compare physicians who perform abortions to Nazi war criminals. Others list the names, addresses, home phone numbers, and other personal information about health professionals who provide abortions. This information is sometimes displayed on-line in the style of "wanted" posters, which accuse the professionals of "crimes against humanity."

For a while, few law-enforcement officials took Internet threats and intimidation seriously. However, after the murders of some abortion providers, it was revealed that their names had been on antiabortion sites that promoted "justifiable homicide." To the creators of these websites, "justifiable homicide" means that it is not wrong to kill anyone who provides abortions. Today, many sites that promote extreme violence against clinics and physicians have been taken down as a result of court orders or the threat of legal action. Still, others are maintained by extreme pro-life groups who believe in so-called justifiable homicide.

Causes of the violence

Violence against clinics is not new. Antiabortion forces have targeted health clinics for decades. This is due in part to a number of factors that, when combined, have made clinics easy targets for antiabortion forces.

In the 1970s, the women's movement was in full swing. Women fought against discrimination and bias. Until that time, women's health care had taken a backseat in the health-care industry. Before *Roe v. Wade*, women who chose to try to get an abortion at a hospital had to ask the hospital directors for permission. Often, these directors, mostly men, denied the procedure. Because of this, many women resorted to illegal and usually unsafe abortions, which put their lives at risk.

When *Roe v. Wade* legalized abortion, women's health-care centers sprang up almost immediately to serve this need. These centers broke away from the restrictive policies of local hospitals and frequently provided abortions. For the first time, women had control over their health-care options. This move was seen by many as a step forward.

As the years passed, however, these clinics became the focus of violent attacks. Many were in freestanding buildings or had space in regular office buildings rather than being part of a hospital, and were well-known in their communities as places where abortions were performed. The employees could be easily identified—unlike in a hospital, where dozens of employees provide a variety of ser-

vices. Therefore, it was relatively easy for a group of abortion foes to surround a clinic and block access. Instead of being a safe haven for women as they had been in the past, clinics became besieged with protesters.

These protesters often represented a new, and sometimes terrifying, group of antiabortion activists, which was another factor in the rise of clinic violence. The late 1980s and early 1990s saw a rise in evangelical and fundamentalist Christianity in the United States. Those who follow these beliefs take the words of the Bible literally, and some of them felt they were called by God to use any means necessary to stop the evil of abortion. Believers by the thousands flocked to women's health clinics to participate in clinic blockades and other forms of intimidation. A number of these people were drawn to the movement by Randall Terry. The organization he founded, Operation Rescue, is thought by some to be responsible for much of the violence that clinics now face.

A common tactic of antiabortion protesters is to surround women's health-care clinics, block access, and intimidate the employees and patients.

The rise of Operation Rescue

Operation Rescue became known for its large, emotionally charged clinic blockades in the late 1980s. Terry founded this national organization in Binghamton, New York, in 1987. He fervently believed that it was the responsibility of all Christians to stop abortion. The first blockades Terry organized succeeded in gaining media attention, and he used this opportunity to spread his message around the country. His efforts drew many evangelical Christians into the organization, and Operation Rescue soon became linked with the growing evangelical Christian movement.

In the book *Beyond Pro-Life and Pro-Choice*, author Kathy Rudy described Terry and his religious beliefs:

> Terry connected his own conversion and personal commitment to Jesus Christ to his growing concerns about abortion and preached an evangelically oriented antiabortion message wherever and however he could. By claiming that God requires evangelical Christians to stop abortion, he . . . paved the way for evangelicalism to dominate antiabortion activities.[10]

Terry, an unassuming-looking man, was a gifted speaker. He took many religious leaders to task for not getting involved in protesting abortion. He believed that the law of God overruled the laws of the United States. He was prepared to break secular law for his beliefs, and he encouraged others to follow him. His single-minded devotion to what he called "saving babies" fired many into action.

In the conservative climate of the United States in the 1980s, Terry was in the right place at the right time. He became a household name almost overnight. In the words of authors James Risen and Judy Thomas,

> [Terry] became the most visible symbol of the loud and unapologetic wing of the newly muscular Religious Right, the leader of a youthful Evangelical legion that saw itself as nothing less than an earthly warning of the coming wrath of God. . . . Terry galvanized Evangelicals by summoning up dark, apocalyptic visions of America.[11]

Soon Operation Rescue chapters were formed in other states, and their self-described rescues became regular events at health clinics nationwide. In many cases, people from all over the country would travel to a specific clinic to be a part of a "rescue."

The tactics that Operation Rescue used during a "rescue mission" were very specific. Terry openly advocated tactics such as breaking into clinics and creating human barriers to prevent patients and employees from entering clinics. He described how the organization prepared for a mission:

> During a rescue mission, the rescuers peacefully but physically place themselves between the killer [the abortion provider] and his intended victim. This is done in a number of ways. They may enter the abortion procedure rooms before the patients arrive and lock themselves in. They may fill up the waiting room or they may come before the abortuary [clinic] opens and block the door with their bodies, their cars or special locks, so that no one can get in. It can be quite exciting and a little frightening.[12]

Although these protests were billed as peaceful, in many cases they were anything but. Antiabortion forces yelled and screamed at women through bullhorns or shouted prayers and Bible verses to intimidate them. Blockades physically

Randall Terry (foreground) and members of Operation Rescue block the entrance to a Planned Parenthood office in New York in 1989.

prevented women from approaching clinic doors. Volunteers who tried to help women pass through the angry crowds were kicked, bitten, and pushed. Protesters swarmed around cars that entered a clinic parking lot, plastering large, graphic color images of what they claimed were aborted fetuses on the drivers' windows and windshields.

The clinics were overwhelmed and frequently unaided by local law enforcement. Many law-enforcement officials were sympathetic to Operation Rescue's cause and refused to break up blockades, claiming that the organization was conducting lawful, peaceful protests. In some cases, the police worked with Operation Rescue to allow the blockades. Occasionally, the police would let Operation Rescue block a clinic for hours before they made any arrests. Since many local police were antiabortion advocates, they saw it as their God-given duty to enable the protests to take place.

Operation Rescue used graphic, full-color images they claimed were of aborted fetuses to intimidate clinic patients.

Few Americans understood the violent underpinnings of these events, so in some cases, it was difficult for pro-choice organizations to garner community support against the blockades. Instead, pro-choice advocates fought back in the courts. In 1992, Marne Greening, the director of the Women's Pavilion in South Bend, Indiana, testified before the Subcommittee on Crime and Criminal Justice about some of the tactics that pro-life groups used against her clinic:

Pro-choice activists also began demonstrating in front of clinics to help ensure safe passage for employees and patients.

> Three women posing as patients were admitted into the clinic for scheduled appointments. One of their partners asked if he could go outside for a moment. When he knocked to reenter, protesters stormed the door, shoved clinic employees aside, and chained themselves throughout the entire clinic with kryptonite locks. Patients already inside the clinic took refuge inside one of the bathrooms and under a desk.[13]

The fall of Operation Rescue and the rise of extreme violence

Until the early 1990s, Operation Rescue was one of the most powerful social and political organizations in the country. Randall Terry was a celebrity. Slowly, however, the antiabortion tide turned. A number of factors contributed to the fall of Operation Rescue and the rise of more militant forms of antiabortion violence.

Many people who supported Operation Rescue's mission were chilled by its blatantly violent and intimidating tactics. The motto of the organization, "If you think that abortion is murder, act like it!" was interpreted by some as an open call for extreme violence. Although Operation Rescue officially denounced extreme violence, it was only a matter of time, some believed, before the demonstrations caused more serious forms of violence. Many moderates who advocated nonviolent protests left the organization.

In 1992, the decision in the case of *Planned Parenthood v. Casey* upheld legal abortions but allowed some restrictions on abortion services. This ruling demoralized Operation Rescue and others in the antiabortion movement because they had hoped the Supreme Court would use the case to strike down *Roe v. Wade* and therefore outlaw abortion.

Law-enforcement officials finally began to crack down on unlawful protests and clinic violence. Many states passed laws prohibiting forms of clinic blockades and violence. Individuals who were arrested during blockades had to pay hefty fines, which convinced many to desert the cause.

The most devastating blow to Operation Rescue came when the organization was taken to court and ordered to pay more than $1 million in damages for its actions against clinics. In the mid-1990s, the organization fizzled out and Randall Terry stepped down as its leader. Operation Rescue still exists, with national headquarters now in Texas, but its power to close clinics and promote violence throughout the United States has waned. It was clear that the years of violence and blockades had not worked.

Although Operation Rescue had not officially condoned serious violence such as bombings and killings, it indirectly supported those who felt more extreme forms of violence were called for. As historian Rickie Solinger makes clear,

> By the end of the 1980s, OR [Operation Rescue] had become the umbrella sheltering extremists who shared a commitment

to uncompromising interventionist tactics and absolutist Christian ideology. For this new style of right-to-lifer . . . They were succeeding by immediately disrupting abortion services and gaining media attention for their cause, amplifying their small numbers through dramatic tactics.[14]

To the more extreme antiabortion believers, victories of the pro-choice movement became the catalyst for a new, terrifying wave of clinic violence.

Fringe groups continue the battle

With the decline of Operation Rescue, many people who were against abortion felt that they had nowhere to go for their voices to be heard. Slowly, other, more extreme antiabortion groups began to fill the gap. An article in the November 9, 1998, issue of *Newsweek*, said, "Since Operation Rescue, which emphasized protest over terror, fell apart in the early '90s, the anti-abortion movement has fractured—and some of the splinter groups like the American Coalition of Life Activists openly promoted violence."[15]

These militant organizations attracted zealous antiabortion believers. Most of these people considered themselves to be devout Christians with a calling to rid the world of

With the help of new state laws prohibiting clinic blockades and violence, police began to take more action against protesters than they had in the past.

abortion. As Frederick Clarkson said in his article, "Anti-abortion Violence: Two Decades of Arson, Bombs, and Murder," "Those who have always advocated some violence have become increasingly revolutionary, seeing themselves as fighters of a holy war to recreate society. . . . Today, those in the most militant wing of the anti-abortion movement are more and more willing to kill."[16]

The most radical of these groups is a shadowy organization known only as the Army of God. This loosely organized group has claimed responsibility for a number of violent acts, including kidnappings and bombing attacks on abortion clinics. In the 1980s, the Army of God published a manual of terrorism that details ninety-nine ways to stop abortion—including arson, bombing, use of acid and other chemicals—and instructions for making explosives.

Other organizations, including the Lambs of Christ, Pro-Life Virginia, Pro-Life Action Network, and others, condone violence against clinics and health-care workers. Their followers are usually radical evangelical Christians, and few mainstream organizations approve of their actions. However, some people believe that these extremists are secretly supported by others in the antiabortion movement.

Paul Hill killed an abortion doctor and the doctor's clinic escort and defended his actions as justifiable homicide.

Reactions to the violence: Who is responsible?

Violence against clinics and abortion providers rose to new heights in the early 1990s with a series of shootings. In 1993, Dr. David Gunn of Florida was killed and Dr. George Tiller of Wichita, Kansas, was shot in both arms. Paul Hill shot and killed Dr. John Britton and his unarmed escort, retired Air Force Lieutenant Colonel James Barrett, outside the Ladies' Center in Pensacola, Florida, in 1994. In 1998, Dr. Barnett A. Slepian, who performed abortions, was struck by a sniper's bullet and killed in his home.

Ironically, Dr. Slepian had written a letter to the *Buffalo News* in 1994, after the death of Dr. Britton. He seemed to be predicting his own murder as he detailed the kinds of harassment that had been directed at him:

> [Protesters] scream that I am a murderer and a killer when I enter the clinics at which they "peacefully" exercise their First Amendment right of freedom of speech. . . . They may also do the same . . . at a restaurant, at a mall, in a store, or, as they have done recently, while I was watching my young children play. . . . But please don't feign surprise, dismay, or certainly not innocence when a more volatile and less-restrained member of the group decides to react to their inflammatory rhetoric by shooting an abortion provider. They all share the blame.[17]

Slepian's letter touches on the core question of abortion violence: responsibility. For years, pro-choice advocates insisted that the hate-filled rhetoric of the antiabortion movement would someday inspire someone to commit murder. Those on the pro-life side of the debate maintained just as strongly that their words were just that: words. They were not responsible, they said, for the extreme actions of a few individuals.

The truth lies somewhere in the middle. Repeatedly, some religious organizations would use inflammatory rhetoric to decry abortion, then refuse to denounce violence completely. This confusing mixed message was interpreted by some as permission to continue violent acts. As Marcy J. Wilder explains in her essay "Law, Violence, and Morality":

> Although many anti-choice organizations have explicitly condemned homicide, other violence including death threats, bombings, arson, acid attacks, and stalking have gone undenounced. Anti-choice leaders . . . maintain a stunning silence on the almost nineteen hundred reported acts of violence and the eleven thousand acts of disruption committed against abortion providers since 1977.[18]

Mark J. Pelavin, associate director of the pro-choice Religious Action Center of Reform Judaism, used even stronger terms to denounce the violence: "This attempt to intimidate women from exercising their constitutional rights should be condemned by all people of conscience.

In Pensacola, Florida, members of NOW (the National Organization for Women) mourn the loss of Dr. David Gunn, Dr. John Britton, and clinic escort James Barrett.

While principled people may disagree about the morality of abortion, using violence as a method of disagreement is morally reprehensible."[19]

Some people view the use of violence to stop abortion as a moral act and matter of conscience. Many conservative Christians believe strongly that God's will must be followed at all costs. If a charismatic leader uses words to suggest that violence is the will of God, some listeners will take those words to heart. It would be, in their minds, a sin to do otherwise. Although a leader might not spread an overt message of murder, a follower might reasonably interpret those words as a call to violence.

This combination of silence and rhetoric created an atmosphere in which some people could see the killing of abortion providers as justifiable homicide. Most who have been convicted of such murders consider themselves to be devoutly religious. Some of them, and their supporters, still see their actions as condoned by God and "justifiable homicide" as a part of the agenda to stop abortions.

Most antiabortion organizations, however, realize that overt violence makes the movement appear to be filled with senseless killers. Many members of these organizations, while committed to ending abortion, decry extreme clinic violence. Gary Bauer, president of the Family Research Council, said in a press release following the bombings in Alabama:

> Once again, an abortion clinic has been bombed. This time, the explosions which ripped through the clinic in Birmingham, Alabama, killed one person and injured another. It is vitally important that all pro-life people speak out clearly and unmistakably to denounce such lawless violence. These actions do violence not only to their intended targets but also to the pro-life cause. . . . No pro-life goal can ever be achieved through bloody acts like these.[20]

Violence takes its toll

In recent years, the most extreme forms of violence against clinics and clinic workers have decreased, partly as a result of the Freedom of Access to Clinics Act, passed by Congress in 1994. The law protects physicians and patients at abortion clinics and established stiff penalties for anyone who breaks the law.

However, some pro-life organizations have claimed that the law violates their free speech rights because they can no longer approach a person entering a clinic to talk to them about abortion. Some states have enacted "safety-zone" laws that specify how close a so-called sidewalk counselor can get to a patient. One state, Colorado, enacted a law that prohibited people from counseling, distributing leaflets, or displaying signs within eight feet of others without their consent whenever they are within one hundred feet of a clinic entrance. This law was challenged by antiabortion groups and eventually went to the Supreme Court.

In June 2000, the Supreme Court handed down a six-to-three ruling upholding the Colorado law and effectively allowing states to pass laws limiting "sidewalk counseling." In the ruling, the Court decided that the right to avoid unwanted communication sometimes outweighs free speech rights. Also, the laws restricting sidewalk counseling are not, in the Court's opinion, aimed at the content of someone's speech. Rather, the laws seek to regulate where, when, and how a message is delivered.

Regardless of the decrease in violence and the legal victories by the pro-choice side, it seems that antiabortion advocates have indeed achieved many of their goals. Today, almost 90 percent of U.S. counties do not have an abortion provider. The extreme violence has driven many physicians and health-care workers from their jobs, for fear of their lives. People who wish to open new clinics have a difficult time finding someone willing to rent them office space, for fear of bombings and attacks. Some clinics that have been damaged or destroyed by violence have not reopened. High insurance premiums as a result of violence deter established physicians from performing abortions. The threat of personal intimidation and other violence keeps medical school graduates from opening new practices to provide abortion services. Older physicians who do perform abortions cannot find younger doctors to replace them when they retire. Whether directly or indirectly, clinic violence has accomplished its intended aim of reducing women's access to abortion.

3

Minors and Abortion: Privacy, Competency, and a Parent's Right to Know

BECKY BELL WAS, by most accounts, a normal, healthy seventeen-year-old girl. She lived in Indianapolis with her parents, attended high school, and looked forward to a bright future. In 1988, Becky became pregnant. Afraid to tell her parents, she went to a local clinic to have an abortion. There she was told that Indiana had a parental notification law. According to the law, minors could not get an abortion unless one parent was told about it. The law also said that if a minor did not want to tell a parent, she could appear in front of a judge to explain why not. The judge might grant her permission for the abortion.

It is clear that Becky left the clinic in good health. For reasons that are still unknown, she decided not to go before a judge. A few days later she became very ill and was taken to a hospital, where she died. An autopsy revealed that Becky had died of pneumonia and the effects of an incomplete abortion. From the evidence, it was suspected that she either got an illegal abortion or tried to perform one herself. Becky's parents were devastated. They blamed Indiana's parental notification law for their daughter's death, believing that if she had been able to get a safe, legal abortion without telling them, she would still be alive today.

Although Becky died more than a decade ago, her story continues to be used as an extreme example of the effects of restrictive parental notification laws that some states have enacted. Since Becky's death, the Bells have repeatedly spoken out against parental notification and consent laws. They have appeared before Congress to express their views, and they continue to urge people to remember Becky's death as a tragic result of laws that kept her from seeking a safe, legal abortion.

People on the antiabortion side of the debate have tried to discredit the Bells and their story. People have suggested that Becky was a wild, promiscuous drug user who somehow deserved her fate. They scoff at the official cause of her death, claiming that she died of an untreated miscarriage rather than an illegal abortion. They hold up her story as evidence that the pro-choice movement fabricates stories to support its views.

Regardless of who is right, Becky's story is a tragedy. Her fate has been wound up in a larger debate—the question of privacy for reproductive decisions, the ability of minors to make competent decisions about abortion, and the role of parents in a minor's abortion choice.

Parents, daughters, and abortion

A minor's right to an abortion has long been a thorny issue in the abortion debate. One of the biggest issues has been what role, if any, parents should play in this decision. Many on the antiabortion side of the debate insist that, as the adult legally responsible for the welfare of the minor, a parent or guardian must be told of a girl's abortion.

This was certainly not the attitude when *Roe v. Wade* legalized abortions in 1973. At that time, abortion became legal for everyone—minors as well as adults. States that had parental consent laws could no longer enforce them. In 1976, the Supreme Court reaffirmed this by ruling that states could not require that a minor obtain parental consent before she got an abortion.

After that, however, the political climate in the United States changed. In the 1980s, political and religious con-

servatives began to promote the so-called family values agenda in politics. These conservatives believed that parents should have ultimate control over their families and that minors were not mentally or emotionally ready to make decisions without their parents. Antiabortion advocates began challenging the laws giving minors the right to have an abortion.

Nancy Bloomer, executive director of the Idaho Christian Coalition, voices her opinion about parental consent for abortion for minors at the Idaho Statehouse in Boise in January 2000.

This changing attitude in the abortion debate peaked in a landmark 1992 Supreme Court decision, *Planned Parenthood v. Casey.* In that decision, the court ruled that a state could require that parents be notified or give their consent before a minor daughter's abortion. They included a judicial bypass option, so that a girl could ask a judge for an abortion instead of involving her parents.

Since then, almost every state has enacted parental notification or consent laws, to the dismay of many pro-choice advocates. However, surveys have suggested that most Americans approve of these laws and other restrictions on a minor's right to obtain an abortion. Even some staunch pro-choice supporters have a hard time arguing against a parent's right to know. This conflict has kept the topic of parental notification and consent laws at the forefront of the abortion debate.

The difference between notification and consent

A majority of the abortion laws that target minors require that a young woman's parents either be notified of a minor's abortion or give their permission for the abortion to take place. Parental notification laws in most states require a medical professional to tell the parent of a minor that she intends to have an abortion. Parental consent laws state that one or both parents must give permission before

a minor can have an abortion. In almost all states where notification or consent laws are on the books, there is also a judicial bypass option. This option gives a minor the right to appear before a judge to explain why she does not want to involve her parents in the abortion decision.

Since each state is allowed to make its own laws regarding abortion for minors, there is now a confusing hodgepodge of laws throughout the country. Some states have no judicial bypass option. Others require counseling, written consent, and other restrictions. A few states, such as New York, have no restrictions on a minor's ability to seek an abortion.

What does this mean for a minor who wants an abortion? It depends on which state she lives in and what her specific circumstances are. Since 1992, there is no longer any guarantee that she will be able to obtain an abortion in her state, even though abortion is legal. Because she is not yet eighteen, her right to choose is severely limited.

A pregnant minor's access to abortion depends on the laws of the state in which she lives.

A minor's right to privacy

One of the central conflicts around notification and consent laws is a teen's right to privacy versus the right of parents to know what their children are doing. The right for adults to have privacy is very clear-cut. However, courts have determined that minors under the age of eighteen do not have the same privacy rights as adults. For example, teens do not always have the right to seek some medical care privately. Many schools and health-care facilities cannot treat or distribute medications to minors without parental permission.

Many psychologists and health-care professionals believe that privacy is vital to a young adult's development. During the teen years, a person grows from a child to an adult, and many teens will go to great lengths to protect their privacy. But parents frequently have a difficult time with the idea that their teens have a right to privacy. They feel anything their child does is their business.

Most in the antiabortion movement argue in favor of a parent's right to be involved in decisions that affect a minor. They feel that a parent's right to know is more important than a teen's right to privacy. For them, notification and consent laws protect parental rights. They point to the fact that parents might have important health information about the family or the minor's medical history that the girl might not. Forcing a pregnant teen to tell her parents about her situation, they argue, will ensure that whatever decision is made will be in the best interest of the teen.

Pro-choice advocates disagree. They stress that because the issue of privacy is so important to minors, notification or consent laws might actually endanger teens. When a teen reveals a pregnancy to her parents, she is also admitting to being sexually active—which can be embarrassing, or even dangerous, if a parent is violent. She may risk her health or her life by having an illegal abortion to avoid having to tell her parents. She might commit suicide or try to bear the child alone. The American Medical Association commented:

> Because the need for privacy may be compelling, minors may be driven to desperate measures to maintain the confidentiality of their pregnancies. They may run away from home, obtain a "back alley" abortion, or resort to self-induced

abortion. The desire to maintain secrecy has been one of the
leading reasons for illegal abortion deaths since . . . 1973.[21]

Many in the antiabortion camp ignore the powerful effects of embarrassment and the wish for privacy when they
advocate notification and consent. Instead, many prefer to
paint every American family as one headed by loving, nur-
turing parents who have their child's best interests at heart.
The reality is that some teens face incest, abuse, and ne-
glect at home. Pregnant teens who come from dysfunc-
tional families might fear more abuse, or a parent might
have threatened to throw them out of the house if they become pregnant. The privacy to choose abortion is even more
important in these situations. The late Judge Nanette Dem-
bitz described some of these realities, saying that a few
mothers deny their daughters' abortions because:

> [They] express a vengeful desire to punish the daughter for
> her sexual activity by making her suffer an unwanted child, a
> fervor to impose a religious conviction the mother has failed
> to instill in her daughter, a hope for caring for the daughter's
> baby as her own because of an inability or unwillingness to
> bear another child for herself, a defensive or resentful attitude
> because [the mother] bore illegitimate children without seek-
> ing or being able to secure an abortion, or a general distaste
> for abortion.[22]

Sometimes the parent's wishes are so contrary to the minor's that communication and agreement is impossible. An
ironic effect of the notification and consent laws have been
cases in which parents have used court orders to make their
daughters have abortions. In one case, a court issued an order of protection against a mother who tried to force her
daughter to have an abortion. The judge acknowledged that
since the decision to have an abortion is protected by the
right of privacy, the decision to have a child is protected by
that right as well.

In some states, the laws mandate that both parents must
be notified or give consent to an abortion. For families in
which one parent is abusive, missing, or incarcerated, this
can be a gigantic obstacle. Many parents of pregnant teens
become furious when they are told that they must track

down a missing or abusive spouse to ask their consent, especially when that spouse is not a part of the teen's life. For these people, the notification and consent laws cause more harm to an already painful situation. Pro-choice advocates admit that these situations are rare, but they maintain that a right to make a private decision about abortion is even more important in these cases than in others. Many antiabortion advocates, however, say these events are so rare as to be insignificant in comparison with a parent's right to know what a child is doing.

Some observers believe that notification laws are part of a larger agenda. Many antiabortion organizations who push for these laws include very religious members who believe that premarital sex is sinful and that it is their moral duty to prevent teens from engaging in such behavior. Not only do these activists oppose abortion, they also oppose allowing minors access to contraceptives and sex-education counseling. Because of this, some critics say that the true purpose of notification and consent laws is not to keep parents informed of their children's lives but to prevent teens from having sex to begin with.

Is a minor competent to choose abortion?

Some antiabortion organizations argue that minors are unable to consider the available options or the effects of the abortion with the same maturity that an adult would. They believe that a teen is generally not capable of making such a serious decision on her own. In the book *The New Civil War: The Psychology, Culture, and Politics of Abortion*, a team of psychologists explains: "Parental consent legislation for minors implicitly or explicitly assumes that protective legislation is necessary because a) abortion carries with it substantial risk, and b) adolescents are incapable of making informed decisions regarding these risks."[23]

Notification and consent laws serve to help teens, antiabortion advocates say, by making sure a competent adult is part of the decision-making process. Statistics suggest that while younger teens may need guidance, older teens are often aware of the implications of their decisions.

Those who support parental consent legislation argue that minors are not capable of making an informed decision without the guidance of an adult.

Although studies have indicated that many teens are just as competent as adults to make rational decisions such as whether to have an abortion, in states that have notification and consent laws, all children are assumed to be incompetent unless proven otherwise. On the question of abortion, the only legal way that a teen can get the procedure in these states without telling her parents is to prove her competency by asking a judge for an abortion.

Judicial bypass: getting a judge's permission

During a judicial bypass hearing, the minor must convince a judge that she is mature enough to make the abortion decision on her own. If she cannot show that she is competent to make this decision, the judge can deny her an abortion. In theory, if she can show her maturity, the judge allows her to have a legal abortion. However, in recent years, it has become apparent that the judicial bypass option is often more of a deterrent than a help—just what many in the antiabortion movement hoped for.

On the surface, this restriction seems reasonable for minors who seek to end their pregnancies without involving their parents, and in fact, most judges allow the girl to have an abortion. But in a number of states, antiabortion judges refuse to grant permission, no matter how competent the minor appears to be. In an article in *The Nation*, writer Amy Bach describes this situation:

> In many of the forty-two states that now have parental notification laws, antiabortion judges have been highly creative when faced with pregnant minors who want their consent for abortions; using harassing interrogation tactics, appointing anti-choice attorneys to represent the young women, and even—in a few cases whose implications are unfolding—assigning lawyers to represent the interest of the fetuses.[24]

Some judges, such as Mark Anderson in Montgomery, Alabama, have openly declared themselves to be antiabortion. Anderson stated that he believes abortion is wrong and routinely denied abortions to minors who sought a judicial bypass. He was also one of the first judges to appoint a lawyer to represent a fetus.

In a case that drew statewide attention, a seventeen-year-old went before Anderson to seek an abortion. She was a high-school honors student who had been awarded a college scholarship. Although she believed that abortion was a sin, she told the court that she thought that any complications from the procedure would be God's punishment. She had been counseled by a pro-life group in the area. She also told the judge that she could not tell her mother about the pregnancy because her mother had threatened to kick her out of the house and give her no help. She also feared violence from her father.

Anderson appointed a lawyer for this young woman's fetus. The lawyer named the fetus "Baby Ashley." Despite a grueling four-hour interrogation by the lawyer, the woman remained calm and steady in her wish to have an abortion. Anderson finally, grudgingly, granted her a bypass.

The local newspapers learned of the story and reported it. Many editorials blasted Anderson, and the public was generally aghast at his blatant tactics. Almost immediately, he stopped being assigned judicial bypass cases. However, antiabortion organizations began to promote the idea of appointing a lawyer to represent the fetus. Soon legislators in Alabama drafted a law to require all judges to appoint a guardian for every fetus of every minor girl who sought a judicial bypass. The bill was eventually defeated in the state legislature, but supporters of the bill vowed to reintroduce it. Legistators in other states have proposed similar laws in their attempts to stop abortions for minors.

Clearly, Anderson and other antiabortion legislators view notification laws as a means to keep young women from having abortions. As the book *The New Civil War: The Psychology, Culture, and Politics of Abortion* states, "Such laws are not intended to protect adolescents from harm. Their real intent is to make abortion more difficult to obtain."[25]

Effects of notification and consent laws

Since the 1992 *Casey* decision enabled most states to enact notification and consent laws, many groups have monitored the effects of the laws on minors and abortion. Some of the more dire predictions about back-alley abortions and suicide have not materialized. Other predictions, on the other hand, have come true.

It seems that the laws do not encourage pregnant teens to talk to their parents any more than they might have if the laws were not in place. Instead, the laws seem to be encouraging them to travel to states that do not have consent or notification requirements to have an abortion. Reporter Timothy J. Vinciguerra describes this trend:

> Predictably, the rates for in-state abortions for minors declined after states adopted these restrictions; however, these states did not experience a corresponding rise in birth rates.

Rather, minor women traveled to adjacent states for their
abortion. The available data suggests that minors who traveled out of state may have accounted for the observed decline
in some states' abortion rates.[26]

Moreover, states adjacent to those that have enacted notification or consent laws saw their abortion rates rise, sup-
porting the idea that minors were traveling to their states
for abortions.

Minors and adults have traveled to other states to secure
abortions since long before *Roe v. Wade* took effect in
1973. However, traveling entails more costs and delays for
minors who may not have the funds or the means of transportation to go out of state. A predictable effect of this is
that minors who travel to other states for abortions usually
have pregnancies that have advanced beyond the first
trimester, when it is safest to perform the procedure. Timothy J. Vinciguerra also noted this fact:

> Abortion providers in the recipient states are often faced with
> the problem of advanced gestation which necessitates proce-
> dures of increased complexity and risk. These young women
> often delay their procedures for reasons of ambivalence, de-
> nial, and inability to acknowledge and deal with the preg-
> nancy. Furthermore, difficulty in gaining information about
> how to obtain and pay for their abortions may also account
> for delayed abortions.[27]

Many minors who are too young to drive or who do not
have the resources to travel out of state sometimes turn to
adults other than their parents for help. In one widely pub-
licized case, a Pennsylvania woman named Rosa Hartford
took a thirteen-year-old girl to New York to get an abortion
without the girl's mother's permission. Eventually the
mother found out about the abortion and Hartford was
prosecuted for interfering with the custody of a minor. She
was convicted and sentenced to one year probation.

Partly as a result of this case, in 1998 Congress introduced the Child Custody Protection Act, also called the
Teen Endangerment Act, which would make it a federal
crime for any person to knowingly transport a minor
across state lines for an abortion if the young woman has
not complied with her home state's law requiring parental

Studies suggest that pregnant minors who live in states with parental consent laws are turning to adults other than their parents and/or traveling outside their state in search of help.

involvement. Predictably, the law met with considerable controversy in Congress. When it was being debated in 1999, antiabortion advocate and House Majority Leader Dick Armey said,

> Grandma has no right to take that child across the state line, circumvent the state laws and dishonor her own children. It is not right to love yourself or love somebody more, or love some abstract devotion to abortion rights more, than the safety and security of that child and the honor of the parents.

In response, Representative David Wu replied: "Young women are better served by talking through the decision and having someone to lean on than going through it alone. This bill would make criminals out of people whose only crime is helping a young woman in distress."[28]

The House and the Senate passed the act, but at the time, President Clinton said that he would sign it only if it was widened to allow family members such as grandparents, siblings, or aunts and uncles to help a minor who needs an abortion. Antiabortion legislators refused to change the law, however, so the legislation stalled.

Do notification laws deter abortions?

Each year, more than one million abortions are performed in the United States. Of those, about 20 percent are performed on minors. In recent years, there has been a dramatic decrease in both teen pregnancy and teen abortion. Both sides of the abortion debate point to parental notification and consent laws as possible causes of the decrease. However, no one knows for sure if these laws have actually resulted in fewer pregnancies and abortions among minors.

Do the laws deter pregnancy? It is not likely. Minors generally do not believe that pregnancy will happen to them until it does happen. Many who choose to use birth control do not use it correctly. Others are coerced into sex or raped. Consent or notification laws have no meaning for these girls until they are already faced with an unwanted pregnancy. For these reasons, the laws probably do little to deter minors from having sex or getting pregnant.

It is clear, however, that these laws do present obstacles in the path of some young women who want an abortion. As more states enact notification and consent laws, it will remain to be seen how much these laws affect the number of abortions to minors. It seems likely, however, that young girls will continue to get abortions in any way they can.

4

The Controversy
Over Partial-Birth
Abortion

ON MARCH 21, 1996, A nurse named Brenda Pratt
Shafer testified before a congressional subcommittee about
a procedure commonly known as "partial-birth" abortion.
This procedure, known in the medical community as intact
dilation and evacuation, had been the focus of intense political and societal debate for a number of years.

Shafer testified that she had worked for three days as a
nurse in an abortion clinic operated by Dr. Martin Haskell,
where she had witnessed the procedure known as a partial-
birth abortion. Although before this experience Shafer had
been pro-choice, the details of the procedure—which she
described—disturbed her. She concluded her graphic testimony with:

> I have been a nurse for a long time and I have seen a lot of
> death—people maimed in auto accidents, gunshot wounds,
> you name it. I have seen surgical procedures of every sort.
> But in all my professional years I have never witnessed any-
> thing like this. . . . I was very much affected by what I had
> seen. For a long time, sometimes still, I had nightmares about
> what I saw at the clinic that day.[29]

Based partly on the strength of Shafer's testimony, Congress introduced legislation to ban partial-birth abortions
on a federal level. Since 1995, thirty state legislatures have
passed laws barring this procedure. The issue of partial-

birth abortions has quickly risen to the forefront of the antiabortion agenda and has become a rallying point for those who want to see both this procedure, and all abortions, outlawed.

What is partial-birth abortion?

Before the 1990s, few had ever heard the term partial-birth abortion. The term is not used by most physicians. However, sometime in the early 1990s antiabortion advocates began using the phrase to describe a specific late-term abortion method known as intact D&E, or dilation and evacuation. During this procedure, the physician partially delivers the fetus feet-first until only the head remains inside the woman. Then the physician inserts a sharp instrument into the back of the fetus's head and makes a hole. The physician inserts a suction device to collapse the head so that the fetus can be removed safely.

The first mention of this method of abortion was in a medical paper delivered by Dr. Martin Haskell at the National Abortion Federation Risk Management Seminar on September 13, 1992. Haskell told his audience that he had developed the procedure as a safer method of performing second- and third-trimester abortions. Soon, other physicians began using Haskell's technique, with positive results.

This technique was considered much safer than the two late-term abortion procedures doctors already used. One, known as classic dilation and extraction, is accomplished by dismembering the fetus inside the uterus with instruments and removing the pieces. The other, called the induction method, is performed when a doctor injects a drug into the uterus to kill the fetus, then delivers the dead fetus.

Both of these procedures carry many risks. A doctor might accidentally tear or cut the uterus during a classic D&E, causing damage and infection. Injecting the uterus with drugs also carries the risk of infection. Any uterine damage or infection can potentially rob a woman of the ability to bear children afterward. If the woman already suffered from a serious medical condition, complications from a late-term abortion could prove life-threatening or fatal.

The abortion method known as intact dilation and evacuation (D&E) was developed to reduce the risks to a woman's health and to her ability to have another child.

However, the intact D&E procedure seemed to reduce these risks to the mother's health and ability to have another child. Since the doctor did not insert any sharp instruments into the uterus, there was little chance of injury to the woman. Because the doctor did not inject drugs directly into the uterus through the abdomen, the danger of infection was lessened. To many in the medical community, this new abortion method was a welcome addition to their practices.

Why women undergo intact D&E

It is estimated that only a small percentage of all abortions in the United States are partial-birth abortions. There is little information in the United States about the number of intact D&E abortions done each year, which makes it difficult for politicians and physicians to know exactly why women choose this method. However, the Alan Guttmacher Institute released a study of women who obtained third-trimester abortions at a Paris hospital between 1986 and 1994. More than half of these sought late abortions because of fetal abnormalities. Most of them had not sought an earlier abortion because they simply did not know about the problems until their pregnancies were advanced.

The reasons that women wait until the second or third trimester to terminate their pregnancies are complex. Some women choose to abort a fetus that has severe physical or mental abnormalities. Others discover that they have a serious medical condition that carrying a pregnancy to term would worsen. Others have difficulty raising money, traveling, and satisfying their state's counseling and notification laws so that by the time they are able to get an abortion, their pregnancies have progressed past the first trimester. Some women, especially minors, deny their pregnancies to themselves until they are too far along for a first-trimester procedure. Rarely, an emergency situation requires that a pregnant woman undergo a late-term abortion to save her life.

Many antiabortion advocates disagree with most medical reasons for a late-term abortion. While they admit that a few women might have serious medical reasons to terminate an advanced pregnancy, most insist that women undergo intact D&Es because of laziness or convenience. A few even believe that no fetus should be aborted, for any reason. These antiabortion advocates insist that even a mother's health is not as important as the life of the fetus, regardless of the situation.

Some women have come forward with their stories of the reasons why they chose intact D&E to terminate their pregnancies. Their experiences indicate that, for most women, ending a wanted pregnancy is a heartrending experience no matter what the reason. This contradicts the antiabortion view that women undergo late-term abortions casually or for the sake of convenience.

Coreen Costello, a mother of two children, testified in Congress about her experience. Costello was a pro-life Re-

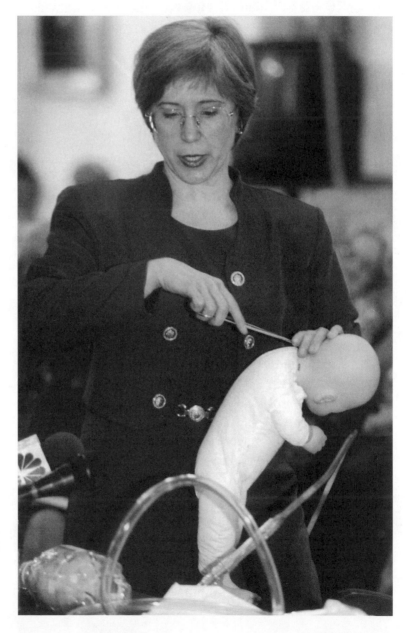

Dr. Kathi Aultman demonstrates a partial-birth abortion on a doll before the House Health and Welfare Committee in Montpelier, Vermont.

publican who was pregnant with a girl she called Katherine. During her seventh month of pregnancy, she was told that the baby had a serious neurological disorder and was not expected to live. Costello described what happened next:

> I considered a Caesarean section, but experts were adamant that the risks to my health and possibly life were too great. There was no reason to risk leaving my children motherless if there was no hope of saving Katherine. The doctors all agreed that our only option was the intact D&E procedure. I was devastated. The thought of an abortion sent chills down my spine.[30]

Another woman, Vicki Wilson, also testified. She was thirty-six weeks pregnant when she discovered that her much-wanted child had severe abnormalities. Wilson explained how she and her husband came to the agonizing decision to have an abortion:

> The biggest question for me and my husband was not "Is she going to die?" A higher power had already decided that for us. The question now was "How is she going to die?" We wanted to help her leave this world as painlessly and peacefully as possible, and in a way that protected my life and health and allowed us to try again to have children.[31]

In both of these cases, the women eventually had other children. Their stories suggest that intact D&E is a procedure that can help to save a mother's life or to ensure that her health is maintained.

The debate becomes emotional

Soon after physicians began using the intact D&E procedure, the antiabortion community began using this late-term abortion method as a vehicle in their quest to make all abortions illegal. They coined the term "partial-birth abortion" because the fetus is partially delivered during the procedure. They began a systematic campaign to portray the procedure in the worst possible light while focusing on the fact that most fetuses that are aborted with this procedure are viable, which means they could survive on their own outside the uterus. For these antiabortion advocates, partial-birth abortion is nothing less than infanticide, or the murder of an infant.

The antiabortion community maintains that partial-birth abortions (intact D&E procedures) are infanticide.

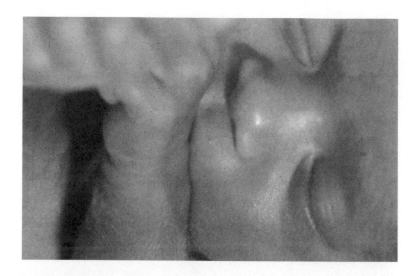

Although most physicians and pro-choice advocates agree that the term "partial-birth" is an inaccurate description of the procedure, antiabortion advocates used this term to increase support for their views among the American public. They showed graphic photos and diagrams of the D&E procedure at court hearings and press conferences. Even staunch pro-choice advocates were uncomfortable and unnerved at the images of a fetus being aborted using this method. In some cases, the physicians who performed the procedure readily admitted that it is unpleasant and difficult. Abortion foes realized the power of the images and of the words and used them to their full extent.

As the controversy over partial-birth abortions moved to the forefront of the abortion debate, pro-choice advocates were ready. Many respected professionals, such as Ron Fitzsimmons, the executive director of the National Coalition of Abortion Providers, stressed that only about 650 D&E abortions were performed a year, and most of them were performed in cases of serious fetal abnormalities or in cases where the mother's health or life were endangered. Pro-choice leaders were confident that the debate would reveal that the antiabortion forces were out of step with the majority of Americans in wanting to ban a safe, necessary procedure.

However, the pro-choice side was unprepared for the power of the images and rhetoric used by antiabortion activists. By continually referring to the fetus as "baby" and "infant," they drew attention away from maternal safety and made it seem as if women had this procedure on a whim. The graphic, disturbing testimonies and photos were highly emotional. Then, in 1995, the pro-choice side was dealt a heavy blow. Ron Fitzsimmons announced that the pro-choice movement had not told the truth about the number of D&E procedures that are done in the United States. He said that he discovered this after talking to physicians around the country about the procedure. He admitted that thousands of these procedures were done annually, not hundreds, as he had originally said. More damaging was his statement that most of the D&E procedures were done in the second trimester on healthy women and fetuses, not on deformed or dead fetuses or mothers who were in danger of dying.

For a while, Fitzsimmons had decided not to speak out. He knew this information would damage the pro-choice position, and he was convinced that keeping intact D&E legal was more important. Eventually, however, he felt compelled to reveal what he knew. Frank and straightforward in his comments, he said, "The pro-choice movement has lost a lot of credibility during this debate, not just with the general public, but with our pro-choice friends in Congress. Even the White House is now questioning the accuracy of some of the information given to it on the issue."[32]

Fitzsimmons blasted the pro-choice leadership for its questionable tactics, but he also said that abortion-rights advocates should never apologize for the use of the procedure. He thought they did that by focusing on only the extreme cases in which a fetus was deformed or a mother's life was endangered. Another pro-choice advocate, Charlotte Taft, explained:

> I think we should put it on the table and say, "OK, this is what we're talking about: when is it OK to end these lives? When is it not? Who's in charge? How do we do it?" These are hard questions, and yet if we don't face them in that kind of responsible way, then we're still having the same conversations we were having 20 years ago.[33]

Referring to the fetus as "baby" and "infant," antiabortion activists used graphic, full-color photos to protest the intact D&E procedure.

Both the pro-choice and antiabortion factions were in an uproar. Pro-choice advocates quickly backpedaled on the issue and denounced Fitzsimmons. Antiabortion forces pointed to his testimony as proof that pro-choice organizations misled the public about the procedure. Some pro-choice leaders had admitted that Fitzsimmons was correct—they had underreported the number of intact D&E procedures. It was a serious political and public relations blunder for the pro-choice position.

In the years following Fitzsimmons' startling revelations, the movement to ban partial-birth abortion roared ahead. Pro-choice advocates scrambled behind, trying to refocus the debate on the lives and health of women. Although they can point to a few victories, it is clear that the antiabortion forces have effectively swayed the American public to their idea of what partial-birth abortions are. A majority of Americans now view partial-birth abortions mainly as an issue of killing a baby rather than saving a mother.

Banning partial-birth abortions as a way to eliminate all abortions

Antiabortion organizations took advantage of the partial-birth controversy at its height in the mid-1990s as a way to change existing abortion law. These organizations, whose purpose is to outlaw all abortions, used the partial-birth question to get many partial-birth bans introduced in Congress and in state legislatures. At first, most of these laws seemed to ban only intact D&E. However, physicians, government officials, and pro-choice organizations began to realize that these laws did much more than ban one specific abortion procedure. The laws were worded so vaguely that they could ban almost every form of abortion, even legal abortions in the first weeks of pregnancy.

This was not a mistake. Some antiabortion groups are clear that this is exactly what they intend. It is their goal to make all abortions illegal, and they have chosen the partial-birth abortion controversy to achieve their goals. Their strategy was for antiabortion legislators to deliberately create vague laws, then pass them under the guise of banning partial-birth abortions. Once the laws were in place, any physician who performed any abortion could be arrested.

In most states, these laws were ruled unconstitutional because of their vague wording. But in other states, the bans were upheld. The law in one state, Nebraska, said,

> Partial birth abortion means an abortion procedure in which the person performing the abortion partially delivers vaginally a living unborn child before killing the unborn child and completing the delivery . . . [This] means deliberately and intentionally delivering into the vagina a living unborn child, or a substantial portion thereof, for the purpose of performing a procedure that the person performing such procedure knows will kill the unborn child and does kill the unborn child.[34]

Many of the thirty states that have enacted, or tried to enact, partial-birth abortion bans had similarly worded legislation. In late 1999, laws in three of these states—Arkansas, Iowa, and Nebraska—were deemed unconstitutional by the U.S. Court of Appeals for the Eighth Circuit. The main reason that they were declared invalid was because they were, in the words of the court, "over inclusive." The ruling explained: "Because both the D&E procedure and the suction-curettage procedure used in second-trimester abortions often include what the Act prohibits, physicians performing those procedures will violate the Act."[35]

In Wisconsin, a ban on partial-birth abortion made it all the way to the State Supreme Court before it was upheld in a close five-to-four decision. One of the judges that voted against it, Chief Judge Richard Posner, said,

> If any fetal lives are saved by these statutes, it will only be by scaring physicians away from performing any late-term abortions. . . . Banning 'partial birth' abortions is not intended to improve the health of women (or anyone, for that matter) it cannot be defended as a health regulation.[36]

He also made a statement about the motives of the anti-abortion movement in this controversy:

> [The statutes] are not concerned with saving fetuses, with protecting fetuses, from a particularly cruel death, with protecting the health of women, with protecting viable fetuses. . . . They are concerned with making a statement in an ongoing war for public opinion . . . That fetal life is more valuable than women's health.[37]

While some antiabortion legislators deny that their intention is to ban all abortions, their actions sometimes suggest otherwise. In many state legislatures and in Congress, pro-choice politicians have attempted to amend the partial-birth laws to give exceptions for the life and health of the mother. Some pro-choice legislators have even publicly announced that they would endorse a partial-birth abortion law with these changes. However, their antiabortion colleagues refuse to make the changes. Most attempts to narrow the laws to focus on intact D&E specifically have been defeated. To many pro-choice legislators, it seems that the antiabortion advocates are deliberately blocking such amendments.

The partial-birth abortion war between pro-choice and antiabortion groups raged in state courts until January 14, 2000, when the U.S. Supreme Court announced that it would consider the constitutionality of the Nebraska ban. And on June 28, the Court handed down a close five-to-

four ruling that struck down the ban on partial-birth abortion, citing that the ban was an "undue burden" on a woman's right to choose abortion.

An antiabortion/pro-choice rally in New York. The controversy continues.

Although it seems as if the ongoing controversy about partial-birth abortions would be ended with the Supreme Court decision, there may be only a pause in the battle. While the Supreme Court justices determined that the Nebraska law did indeed ban other forms of abortion, they seemed to keep the door open for other legislation that would ban the D&E procedure. Justice Sandra Day O'Connor stated that "A ban on partial birth abortion that only proscribed the D&E method of abortion and that included an exception to preserve the life and health of the mother would be constitutional in my view."[38]

People on both sides of the issue are certain that anti-abortion legislators will soon draft new legislation to ban partial-birth abortion that follows the guidelines now set by the Supreme Court. If any new laws include the exceptions stated by Justice O'Connor, it is likely that they will be passed and upheld as constitutional. The debate is far from over.

5

RU 486 and Medical Abortions: A New Twist on the Controversy

IN 1992, A YOUNG, pregnant American woman named Leona Benten stepped off an airplane at JFK Airport in New York. She had just arrived from Europe. She did not seem any different from any other passenger, except for the fact that she was immediately ushered into Customs amid a tight knot of security. Customs officials confiscated pills that the woman was carrying with her. It was a drug known as RU 486, or the "French abortion pill." At that time, the drug was banned in the United States. Benten, with the support of pro-choice organizations, was trying to challenge the law by bringing the pills into the United States with the intent to use them to end her pregnancy. They wanted to call attention to the ban, so they deliberately alerted officials so that the arrest would be covered in the news.

When her case was tried, a federal court ruled in favor of Benten's right to have RU 486, which she had gotten legally overseas. However, the Supreme Court refused to order Customs to return the RU 486 to Benten.

These little white pills represented a huge bombshell for both the antiabortion and pro-choice factions in the United States. RU 486, now more commonly known as mifepristone in the United States, is considered to be the most significant advance in reproductive health since birth-control pills. The drug works by blocking a naturally occurring hormone called progesterone, which is vital to the earliest stages of pregnancy. Progesterone helps build the uterine lining to support the fertilized egg. When the hormone is blocked, the lining breaks down and bleeding occurs. Another drug, misoprostol, then causes the uterus to expel the fertilized egg. This drug combination is more than 90 percent effective in women whose pregnancies are less than seven weeks along.

People on both sides of the abortion question realized that RU 486 would dramatically change the debate in the United States by redefining the way that abortions are performed. For pro-choice advocates, RU 486 was a breakthrough in creating privacy to make a personal abortion decision. Women could get medical abortions from their family physicians rather than at a stand-alone clinic that could be the target of antiabortion protests or violence. No one except a woman and her doctor would ever have to know about the abortion. As writer Marie Bass states in the book *Abortion Wars*,

> Maybe—just maybe—this [RU 486] was a way out of the quagmire of the abortion issue. If such a product were safe and effective and women accepted it, perhaps it could take the abortion issue out of the political arena and put the decision back in the hands of women and medical practitioners, where it belonged.[39]

Antiabortion forces, on the other hand, were alarmed at the idea that medical abortions might become even more widespread than surgical abortions. They feared that without specific targets such as clinics and physicians, it would be more difficult to protest abortions and those who perform them. They claimed that the drug is harmful to women. Both sides vowed to fight.

RU 486 use in Europe

The drug that changed the abortion debate was developed in France in the mid-1980s, and almost from the moment it was released, it was mired in political controversy. In 1988 RU 486, which had been developed by the French pharmaceutical company Roussel Uclaf, was formally approved in France. Only a month later, the world was stunned by the news that Roussel Uclaf had abruptly suspended the sale of the drug, because, as Marie Bass reports, "After enduring repeated protests from the French Catholic Church and anti-abortion groups, Roussel Uclaf had reluctantly concluded that (in the words of Roussel Uclaf president Edouard Sakiz), 'the public is not ready for RU 486.'"[40]

However, another surprising announcement, this one from the French minister of health, came only a month later. According to Marie Bass,

[He] made a simple, elegant statement ordering the drug back onto the market on the grounds that he could not allow the abortion debate to deprive women of a product that represented medical progress. From the moment the government approved the product, he said, it had become "the moral property of women.[41]

Roussel Uclaf obeyed the order to return RU 486 to the market. But from that moment, the company steadfastly refused to market the drug in the United States, where the abortion conflict was even more volatile.

Roussel Uclaf had reason to be squeamish about the controversy. Its parent company, Hoechst A G of Germany, was one of three corporations that emerged from the breakup of I G Farben, the German chemical company that once manufactured the cyanide gas for Nazi death camps. Antiabortion forces had begun comparing RU 486 to the gas that the Nazis used to kill millions of innocent people during World War II, and the company certainly did not want to do anything that would remind people of that time in their history.

In 1989 Hoechst reaffirmed their decision, announcing that they would not market or distribute the drug outside of

French professor Etiennie-Emile Baulieu developed RU 486, the "French abortion pill."

France. Meanwhile, antiabortion organizations in the United States exerted great pressure on the Food and Drug Administration to ban the drug. Finally, the agency responded to the pressure by banning RU 486 for importation to the United States.

Although pro-choice organizations were prevented from bringing the drug to the United States by the ban, they were not idle. Some groups began a public awareness campaign to promote the positive aspects of the drug. Others worked with the medical community to study the drug and to make more physicians aware of its positive applications. They also kept an eye on how RU 486 was faring in Europe.

Slowly, the drug gained acceptance in European countries besides France, although the controversy continued overseas as well. Over the years, more than five hundred thousand women in Great Britain and Europe used the drug to end their pregnancies. Since the drug was so new, people were not sure how well it would work or if women would accept it as a replacement for surgical abortions. To the relief of many U.S. pro-choice groups, European physicians began to report that RU 486 was indeed safe, despite some side effects including bleeding, cramping, and nausea, which are normal reactions to the body expelling the uterine lining. A majority of patients had chosen to use RU 486 rather than undergo a surgical abortion. As the positive reports began coming in, pro-choice groups prepared to battle to get RU 486 approved in the United States. Antiabortion groups were just as determined to keep it out of the country, and they also prepared their fight.

RU 486 and medical abortions in the United States

During the late 1980s and early 1990s, the political climate in the United States was clearly antiabortion. The Reagan and Bush administrations openly denounced abortion in favor of a "right to life" agenda that sought to make all abortions illegal. The government classified RU 486 as a banned drug, which meant that no U.S. studies or trials could be held to determine if it was safe or effective. Congress held hearings about the drug, in which scientists testified that the ban also prohibited them from studying other uses of the drug, including as a possible treatment for breast cancer. Antiabortion groups dismissed these claims, and the ban remained in effect.

The controversy raged on and became one of the deciding factors in the 1992 presidential election. During Bill Clinton's campaign, he promised to support efforts to bring RU 486 into the United States, and his stand for many pro-choice issues helped get him elected. As soon as he was sworn in, he issued an executive order instructing the FDA to reevaluate the RU 486 ban. Pro-choice forces were elated. Finally, they thought, the drug would be available in the United States.

However, this was not to be. At the time, clinic violence and restrictive abortion legislation were common throughout America. Because of the strong antiabortion sentiment, no American manufacturers wanted to touch such a politically charged product as RU 486. Ultimately, in 1994, after intense negotiations with American pro-choice groups, Roussel Uclaf agreed to donate the United States patent rights to the Population Council, a nonprofit reproductive health organization. Since the drug would not be licensed or developed in the United States by Roussel Uclaf, it was decided that it would no longer be called RU 486. Instead, it would be known by its scientific name, mifepristone.

U.S. physicians' response to the controversy

From the moment that RU 486 was in the news, American women began asking for it. However, it was clear that it might take years for RU 486 to be approved in the United States, and this prompted some medical researchers to search for other drugs that might induce abortions. They found one, called methotrexate, which was already in use in the United States. As researchers Linda Beckman and S. Marie Harvey state in the book *The New Civil War: The Psychology, Culture, and Politics of Abortion*,

> This drug has been available in the United States since 1953 and is currently marketed for other uses such as the treatment

of rheumatoid arthritis, cancer and severe psoriasis. In combination with misoprostol, methotrexate has been found to produce a successful early first-trimester abortion in most women.[42]

Starting in the early 1990s, because RU 486 was banned, doctors quietly began prescribing methotrexate to induce abortions, even though the drug was not originally intended for this purpose. For the first time, some physicians who did not perform surgical abortions began offering medical abortions. This was exactly what the pro-choice side had hoped for and what the antiabortion forces feared. Women began having abortions privately, without facing violence and shame.

Soon, however, problems arose. Because so little information existed about medical abortions in the United States, many physicians remained unsure of the procedure. Others were hesitant to try medical abortions because RU 486 had yet to be approved by the FDA and methotrexate was not specifically approved for use in abortions. But doctors were beginning to become more aware of medical abortions, and many began doing research on their own.

The abortion pill, RU 486, is called mifepristone in the United States.

One physician said, "Friends of mine [other physicians] were calling, saying they were doing it, patients were starting to inquire. . . . I saw a lot of people were doing this. . . . So I went back and immediately read the articles that had been published about it, and started doing it."[43]

Part of the confusion came with the perception that medical abortions were quick and easy to do. Antiabortion groups added to the confusion by decrying medical abortion and making it seem as if women only had to take a single pill to end a pregnancy. Some doctors even had the impression that medical abortion was fast and simple.

However, this is not the case. The doctor must determine how far along the pregnancy is, usually by doing an ultrasound procedure, since medical abortions are most effective during the first few weeks of pregnancy. The drugs are taken in stages, over the course of a few days. Patients have to return to the clinic at least once, sometimes twice, for follow-up care.

Patients were also unsure about the exact nature of medical abortions. Women were generally unaware that there would be many uncomfortable effects of a medical abortion, including severe cramping, dizziness, and heavy bleeding as the body expelled the uterine lining. Physicians discovered that they needed to carefully counsel women who were considering this method, more so than for a surgical abortion. It was vital to determine whether a particular woman would psychologically be able to handle the bloody effects of the medical abortion.

Slowly, as more physicians and patients used medical abortions, these questions and concerns were answered. Most doctors reported few complications with medical abortions. Predicted horror scenarios such as women bleeding to death at home or refusing to return for follow-up visits did not occur. Women who used the procedure found it uncomfortable and painful, but careful counseling had prepared them for the effects. Pro-choice groups pointed to these results as proof that RU 486 should be approved, but antiabortion factions used the same data to insist that the bleeding and pain meant that the drugs were harmful.

The controversy continues

As a result of intense lobbying by pro-choice groups, clinical trials of RU 486 began in 1994. During the clinical trials, antiabortion organizations lobbied Congress and state legislators to outlaw the drug. They produced information showing that medical abortions were dangerous to women. The side effects of the drugs, such as the bleeding and nausea, were held up as proof that the drug was dangerous. The pro-choice groups responded by citing the success of the drug in Europe.

In 1996, despite the efforts of the antiabortion community, the Food and Drug Administration (FDA) recommended that the drug be approved. Pro-choice advocates were poised to declare victory. Newspapers and magazines heralded the introduction of the new abortion method. Then the delays began.

Throughout the lengthy FDA approval process, antiabortion groups and politicians had battled against the drug. They threatened pharmaceutical companies with boycotts if they distributed RU 486, resulting in a climate of uneasiness and fear within the drug manufacturing community. No one wanted to be responsible for making and distributing the drug because many extreme antiabortion groups threatened that manufacturing plants would be besieged with protesters or become the targets of violence. Most companies bowed to the pressure, and for some time it seemed as if RU 486 might never go on the market at all. Finally, pro-choice groups convinced a company called the Danco Group to manufacture, distribute, and market the drug in the United States.

But the threat of violence and boycotts remained. Pro-choice advocates feared that although RU 486 would be legal, many drugstore chains and pharmacies would refuse to sell it. To avoid such refusals, it was decided to distribute the drug directly to physicians. Writer Margaret Talbot explained,

> The . . . reason [for distributing the drug directly to physicians] surely, is the likelihood that some individual pharmacists and even some drugstore chains would simply refuse to

dispense [the drugs], as some of them have already refused to dispense Previn, the emergency contraception kit. Wal-Mart, one of the country's biggest pharmaceutical retailers, announced . . . [t]hat it would not sell Previn, and a small but noisy group called Pharmacists for Life International has been pushing for state laws and professional "conscience clauses" protecting druggists who refuse to fill prescriptions for abortifacients and even birth control pills.[44]

After months of waiting, by the beginning of the year 2000, it seemed as if approval was almost certain. Then in February, pro-choice groups were disappointed when the FDA delayed approval once again, due to questions about distribution and manufacture of the drug. There were also rumors that the FDA would request some restrictions on the drug, although no one was sure what they might be.

Despite these rumors, both sides of the debate were shocked when, on June 7, 2000, the press reported that the FDA was prepared to approve RU 486 only with serious restrictions. These restrictions included a national registry of all doctors prescribing the drug, a requirement that those doctors have admitting privileges at a hospital within one hour of their offices, a mandatory follow-up study of all women who have medical abortions, and a rule that allows only doctors who already perform surgical abortions to prescribe the drug.

Pro-choice groups were stunned and furious. Gloria Feldt, president of the Planned Parenthood Federation of America, said, "What the FDA is talking about so violates physicians' privacy and security concerns that mifepristone could be approved by the agency but never really be on the market."[45]

Most of the restrictions suggested by the FDA would have effectively prevented the drug's use as a safe, private alternative to surgical abortion. Pro-choice groups feared that, in the words of Vickie Saporta, director of the National Abortion Federation, "Few [doctors] will be interested in using mifepristone, and the drug's great promise . . . [t]o improve access to women who are seeking early abortion services will be lost."[46]

These fears proved unfounded when, in September 2000, the FDA finally approved RU 486 with relatively few restrictions, saying that clinical trials had shown the drug to be safe and effective. Predictably, pro-choice advocates hailed the move as a major victory for their cause, while abortion foes denounced it. But both sides agreed that although FDA approval would change the abortion debate, it would not end it.

Will medical abortion remove the stigma of abortion?

The long battle over FDA approval of RU 486 highlights the advantages, and the problems, of medical abortion in the United States. Although abortion is legal, it is a difficult decision fraught with moral questions. Many women feel ashamed for choosing abortion, and few women talk about their choice for fear of being seen in a bad light. This is due in part to the unceasing efforts of the antiabortion groups who continually paint abortion in negative terms. They tell women that abortion is wrong and that they are bad people

Antiabortion activists pass out Bibles and antiabortion posters to women who visit abortion clinics to reinforce the message that abortion is wrong and immoral.

for choosing to terminate their pregnancies. Often, women who visit clinics are bombarded with this message by violent antiabortion protesters, exacerbating the feelings of shame and anger. All of these factors have resulted in society considering abortion to be negative and embarrassing. As Carolyn Westhoff, an obstetrician and gynecologist at Columbia University medical school, said, "One of my real, and I think realistic hopes for this method is that it will help get abortion back into the medical mainstream and out of this ghettoized place it's been in."[47]

Pro-choice advocates view RU 486 as a way to remove the stigma from abortion and enable women to choose the procedure without shame. With RU 486, women will no longer be forced to endure the taunts and screams of antiabortion groups as they enter clinics. Their decision to choose abortion would be a private one rather than a public, highly politicized one.

However, the sense that abortion is disgraceful is deeply ingrained in society, and this attitude will change slowly. Even women who support medical abortions may, consciously or unconsciously, be influenced by the attitude—promoted by antiabortion advocates—that only morally loose women get abortions. A study conducted by researchers Linda Beckman and S. Marie Harvey found that

> Many women were concerned that mifepristone would make the abortion procedure too "easy" and would allow "other women" to make a decision to have an abortion without giving it proper thought. This finding also may be due, in part, to the political controversy surrounding abortion in the United States, where in contrast to most developed countries, the morality of abortion remains a highly volatile and contentious issue.[48]

It seems certain that even if medical abortion succeeds in reducing the stigma surrounding abortion, the process will take a very long time.

Will medical abortion make abortion more available?

Besides removing the stigma of abortion, another hoped-for effect of RU 486 is that it will make abortion more read-

Antiabortion demonstrators gather for the annual Right to Life March in Washington, D.C.

ily available to greater numbers of women. Now able to perform abortions privately, doctors would be free from the fear of protests, violence, or death. Observers predict, therefore, that doctors who have never before considered offering abortions will begin doing so in significant numbers.

Some studies indicate that this prediction may come true. In 1998, the Henry J. Kaiser Family Foundation surveyed family doctors about their willingness to use medical abortions once the drugs were approved by the FDA. Almost half said they were likely do so. One family doctor said, "[Medical abortion] feels more natural for a family doctor, giving medication and helping somebody through the side effects. . . . I started doing these in 1993 and now it's more than half of my abortion practice."[49]

Still, there are a number of thorny issues for doctors that may not be resolved by the introduction of medical abortions. For example, many physicians live in communities

76

Pro-choice advocates hope that legalization of RU 486 will curb antiabortion violence, such as the murder of Dr. David Gunn. This woman distributes flyers for his memorial service.

that do not approve of abortions. A number of these doctors refuse to offer abortions because of the threats of violence and intimidation that abortion providers face. In a recent study of health-care providers in rural Washington State, for example, most of them currently do not provide abortion services because of community opposition and moral objection to abortion. It is not likely that the availability of medical abortion will change the moral climate in these communities.

A serious ethical question that doctors may face is whether the women who ask for a medical abortion really understand what it is. Most physicians who perform abortions believe that a woman should not get the procedure unless she has made a free, informed choice. However, many women are so terrified of the disgrace surrounding the termination of a pregnancy that they want to believe that medical abortion is not really "abortion." Doctors have been faced with women who say things like, "I don't believe in abortion, but I can't be pregnant. Give me the pill that will make me stop being pregnant." Clearly, medical abortion has the potential to raise new issues and controversies about abortion.

The future of medical abortion in the United States

Both sides agree that medical abortions will not end the debate over abortion. In spite of the FDA's approval of RU 486, most antiabortion organizations insist that they will continue to protest at clinics and to publicize the names and personal information of doctors who perform medical abortions as well as surgical abortions. The companies that manufacture and distribute the drug will be the focus of their efforts, as well. Jeff White, speaking for the group Operation Rescue West, says, "We intend to target the distributors of this drug, just as we have doctors. We'll do our investigations; we'll find out the names of company executives; we'll go to their neighborhoods."[50]

Perhaps there will come a day when both sides conclude that the battle over abortion will not be completely won by either side. But for the foreseeable future, the battle will continue.

Notes

Chapter 1: What Is Abortion?

1. National Abortion Federation, "What is Surgical Abortion?" (fact sheet), January 2000, p. 1.

2. Quoted in J. Douglas Butler and David Walbert, eds., *Abortion, Medicine, and the Law*. New York: Facts On File, 1986, p. 241.

3. Quoted in Butler and Walbert, *Abortion, Medicine, and the Law*, p. 244.

4. Quoted in Butler and Walbert, *Abortion, Medicine, and the Law*, p. 241.

5. Quoted in Butler and Walbert, *Abortion, Medicine, and the Law*, p. 241.

6. National Abortion Federation, "What is Medical Abortion?" (fact sheet), January 2000, p. 1.

Chapter 2: Clinic Violence and Its Effect

7. Christopher Daly, "Gunman Kills 2, Wounds 5 in Attack on Abortion Clinics," *Washington Post*, December 31, 1994, p. A01.

8. Quoted in James Risen and Judy L. Thomas, *Wrath of Angels: The American Abortion War*. New York: Basic Books, 1998, pp. 120–121.

9. National Abortion Federation, "Testimony of Emily Lyons Before the House Judiciary Committee on Crime," July 17, 1998. www.prochoice.org/violence/emily_lyons.htm.

10. Kathy Rudy, *Beyond Pro-Life and Pro-Choice*. Boston: Beacon Press, 1996, p. 45.

11. Quoted in Risen and Thomas, *Wrath of Angels*, p. 218.

12. Quoted in Rudy, *Beyond Pro-Life and Pro-Choice*, p. 44.

13. National Abortion Federation, "Testimony of Marne Greening Before the Subcommittee on Crime and Criminal Justice," May 6, 1992. www.prochoice.org/violence.greening.htm.

14. Quoted in Rickie Solinger, ed., *Abortion Wars: A Half-Century of Struggle, 1950–2000*. Berkeley and Los Angeles: University of California Press, 1998, p. 232.

15. Quoted in T. Trent Gegax and Lynette Clemetson, "The Abortion Wars Come Home," *Newsweek*, November 9, 1998. dailydavos.com/nw-srv/issue/19_98b/printed/int/us/na0119_1.htm.

16. Frederick Clarkson, "Anti-abortion Violence: Two Decades of Arson, Bombs, and Murder," *Southern Poverty Law Center Intelligence Report*, Summer 1998. www.splcenter.org/intelligenceproject/ip4g2.html.

17. Quoted in Joni Scott, "From Hate Rhetoric to Hate Crime: A Link Acknowledged Too Late," *The Humanist*, January-February 1999, pp. 8–14.

18. Quoted in Solinger, *Abortion Wars*, p. 84.

19. Mark Pelavin, *Religious Action Center Newsletter*, January 29, 1998. www.rj.org/rac/news/012998.html.

20. Family Research Council, "Bauer Denounces Abortion Clinic Bombing," January 29, 1998. www.frc.org/press/012998.html.

Chapter 3: Minors and Abortion: Privacy, Competency, and a Parent's Right to Know

21. Quoted in "The Child Custody Protection Act and the Inadequacy of Judicial Bypass Procedures," September 1998. www.naral.org/publications/facts/bypass_97.html.

22. Quoted in Douglas and Walbert, *Abortion, Medicine, and the Law*, p. 159.

23. Quoted in Linda Beckman and S. Marie Harvey, eds., *The New Civil War: The Psychology, Culture, and Politics of Abortion*. Washington, DC: American Psychological Association, 1998, p. 286.

24. Amy Bach, "No Choice For Teens," *The Nation*, October 11, 1999, p. 7.

25. Quoted in Beckman and Harvey, *The New Civil War*, p. 295.

26. Timothy J. Vinciguerra, "Notes of a Foot Soldier," *Albany Law Review*, Spring 1999, p. 1167.

27. Vinciguerra, "Notes of a Foot Soldier," p. 1167.

28. Quoted in Julie Hirschfeld, "House-Passed Ban on Evasion of Parental Notification Laws Faces Senate Procedural Hurdles," *CQ Weekly*, July 3, 1999, p. 1621.

Chapter 4: The Controversy Over Partial-Birth Abortion

29. House Committee on the Judiciary, Subcommittee on the Constitution, *The Partial-Birth Abortion Ban Act: Hearings on H.R. 1833*, 105th Cong., 1st sess. 1996.

30. Senate Committee on the Judiciary, *The Partial-Birth Abortion Act: Hearings on H.R. 1833*, 104th Cong., 1st sess., 1995.

31. Senate Committee, *The Partial-Birth Abortion Act*.

32. Quoted in Dianc Gianelli, "Abortion Rights Leader Urges End to 'Half-Truths,' " *AMNews*, March 3, 1997. www.ama-assn.org/sci-pubs/amnews/pick_97/spec0303.htm#top.

33. Quoted in Gianelli, "Abortion Rights Leader Urges End to 'Half-Truths.' "

34. *Carhart v Stenberg*, 92 F3d 1142 (8th Cir. 1999), No. 99-830.

35. Quoted in Jennifer Doran, "Constitutional Law: Three Bans on 'Partial-Birth' Abortions Deemed Unconstitutional," *American Journal of Law and Medicine*, Winter 1999, p. 569.

36. *The Hope Clinic et al. v James E. Ryan, Attorney General of Illinois, et al.*, No. 98-1726 (7th Cir., October 26, 1999).

37. *Hope Clinic v Ryan*.

38. Quoted in "Court Nixes Nebraska Abortion Law," *New York Times*, June 28, 2000. www.nytimes.com/aponline/w/PA-Scouts-Abortion.html.

Chapter 5: RU 486 and Medical Abortions: A New Twist on the Controversy

39. Quoted in Solinger, *Abortion Wars*, p. 254.

40. Quoted in Solinger, *Abortion Wars*, p. 257.

41. Quoted in Solinger, *Abortion Wars*, p. 258.

42. Beckman and Harvey, *The New Civil War*, p. 190.

43. Quoted in Carole Joffee, "Reactions to Medical Abortions Among Providers of Surgical Abortion—An Early

Snapshot, Part 1," *Family Planning Perspectives: The Alan Guttmacher Institute Newsletter*, January-February 1999. www.agi-usa.org/pubs/journals/3103599.html.

44. Quoted in Margaret Talbot, "The Little White Bombshell," *New York Times Magazine*, July 11, 1999. www.nytimes.com/library/magazine/home/19990711mag-abortion-pill-html.

45. Mark Kaufman, "Abortion Drug Proposal Criticized," *Washington Post*, June 7, 2000, p. A01.

46. "Mifepristone: FDA Proposes 'Tight' Restrictions for Abortifacient," *Kaiser Daily Reproductive Health Report*, June 7, 2000. http://report.kff.org/archive/repro/2000/06/kr000607.1.htm.

47. Quoted in Talbot, "The Little White Bombshell."

48. Quoted in Joffee, "Reactions to Medical Abortions."

49. Beckman and Harvey, *The New Civil War*, p. 205.

50. Quoted in Talbot, "The Little White Bombshell."

Organizations to Contact

American Life League
P.O. Box 1350
Stafford, VA 22555
(540) 659-4171

The American Life League is a religious organization whose members believe life begins at conception. Its mission statement says that the group exists to "serve God by helping to build a society that respects and protects innocent human life from fertilization to natural death—without compromise, without exception, without apology."

Baptists for Life
P.O. Box 3158
Grand Rapids, MI 49501
(616) 458-9999

The Baptist faith is one of the largest Protestant denominations in the United States, and Baptists for Life works with local churches to develop pro-life ministries. They see abortion as a horror and work to help women choose other alternatives.

Catholics for a Free Choice
1436 U Street NW, Suite 301
Washington, DC 20009-3997
(202) 986-6093

Catholics for a Free Choice is a large organization that has broken away from the standard Catholic beliefs against abortion and birth control. The group is an independent, not-for-profit organization that focuses on education and reproductive health.

National Abortion Federation
1755 Massachusetts Avenue NW, Suite 600
Washington, DC 20036
(202) 667-5881

The National Abortion Federation, one of the most visible pro-choice organizations, was founded in 1977 as a professional association of abortion providers in the United States and Canada. Its main goal is to provide a forum for professionals such as physicians, legal professionals, and reproductive rights organizations that promote abortion rights.

National Right to Life Committee
419 7th Street NW, Suite 500
Washington, DC 20004
(202) 626-8800

NRLC is one of the largest, best-known political organizations promoting pro-life beliefs. *USA Today* once called the NRLC the most powerful pro-life organization in the country. The main objective of this group is to pass pro-life legislation and to lobby Congress to change public policy regarding abortion.

Planned Parenthood Federation of America
810 Seventh Avenue
New York, NY 10019
(212) 541-7800

Founded by Margaret Sanger in 1916, Planned Parenthood is the world's largest and oldest voluntary family planning organization. It is the most recognized organization in the pro-choice movement, with clinics in almost every state and abroad. Planned Parenthood is dedicated to the idea that every individual has a fundamental right to decide when or whether to have a child, and that every child should be wanted and loved. Although many Planned Parenthood clinics do not perform abortions on their premises, they have been the target of much pro-life violence in the past.

Suggestions for Further Reading

Tricia Andryszewski, *Abortion: Rights, Options, and Choices*. Brookfield, CT: Millbrook Press, 1996. This book explores the ethics, funding, and availability of abortion in a clear, easy-to-understand style.

Nancy Day, *Abortion: Debating the Issue*. New Jersey: Enslow Publishers, 1995. The history of abortion and its moral and legal aspects are covered in this easy-to-read book.

Anne Eggebroten, ed., *Abortion: My Choice, God's Grace: Christian Women Tell Their Stories*. Pasadena, CA: Hope Publishing, 1994. The Christian perspective on abortion is explored through the stories of Christian women who have chosen the procedure.

Annrenee Englander, *Dear Diary, I'm Pregnant: Teenagers Talk About Their Pregnancy*. New York, Annik Press, 1997. This collection of first-person accounts includes the experiences of ten teens as they made personal choices about how to deal with their pregnancies.

Kathlyn Gay, *Pregnancy: Private Decisions, Public Debates*. Sherman, CT: Franklin Watts, 1994. Part of the *Women Then and Now* series, this book discusses the many facets of reproductive rights.

Tamara L. Roleff, ed., *Abortion: Opposing Viewpoints*. San Diego: Greenhaven Press, 1997. This book tackles the abortion question from both sides of the debate.

Works Consulted

Books

Linda Beckman and S. Marie Harvey, eds., *The New Civil War: The Psychology, Culture, and Politics of Abortion.* Washington, DC: American Psychological Association, 1998. A series of essays that deal with the psychological and cultural impact of abortion around the world.

J. Douglas Butler and David Walbert, eds., *Abortion, Medicine, and the Law.* New York: Facts On File, 1986. An anthology of articles written by professionals in medicine, law, psychology, and government, this book touches on the legal, ethical, religious, psychological, and medical aspects of abortion.

Rebecca Chalker and Carol Downer, *A Woman's Book of Choices: Abortion, Menstrual Extraction, RU 486.* New York: Seven Stories Press, 1996. This easy-to-read guide includes practical information on abortion laws, clinics, costs, and procedures.

Mark A. Graber, *Rethinking Abortion: Equal Choice, the Constitution and Reproductive Politics.* Princeton, NJ: Princeton University Press, 1999. The author interprets abortion law and suggests new approaches to disarming the abortion debate.

James Davison Hunter, *Before the Shooting Begins: Searching for Democracy in America's Culture Wars.* New York: The Free Press, 1994. This overview of the abortion question focuses on the rise in clinic violence and its possible origins.

Donald P. Judges, *Hard Choices, Lost Voices: How the Abortion Conflict Has Divided America, Distorted*

Constitutional Rights, and Damaged the Courts. Chicago: Ivan R. Dee, 1993. A balanced discussion of abortion issues, including history and the impact of the conflict on society.

Kristin Luker, *Abortion and the Politics of Motherhood*. Berkeley and Los Angeles: University of California Press, 1985. This book takes a hard look at the abortion controversy in the United States from economic, societal, and cultural viewpoints.

———, *Dubious Conceptions: The Politics of Teenage Pregnancy*. Cambridge, MA: Harvard University Press, 1997. A serious look at the politics of teenage pregnancy, emphasizing the complex issues surrounding the country's views of teen motherhood.

David Mall, ed., *When Life and Choice Collide*. Libertyville, IL: Kairos Books, 1994. This collection of scholarly essays discusses language and the abortion controversy.

Sydna Masse and Joan Phillips, *Her Choice to Heal: Finding Spiritual and Emotional Peace After Abortion*. New York: Chariot Victor, 1998. A Christian writer recounts her experiences with abortion and her subsequent belief that abortion is wrong.

Louis P. Pojman and Francis J. Beckwith, *The Abortion Controversy*. Boston: Jones and Bartlett Publishers, 1994. Includes a variety of scholarly articles from all perspectives of the abortion debate.

James Risen and Judy L. Thomas, *Wrath of Angels: The American Abortion War*. New York: Basic Books, 1998. This book chronicles the rise of the antiabortion movement, its role in the creation of the Religious Right, and the impact of violence in the antiabortion movement.

Kathy Rudy, *Beyond Pro-Life and Pro-Choice*. Boston: Beacon Press, 1996. An insightful, complete overview of abortion and the religious, moral, and philosophical aspects of the debate.

Rickie Solinger, ed., *Abortion Wars: A Half-Century of Struggle, 1950-2000*. Berkeley and Los Angeles: University of California Press, 1998. This volume includes the opinions of a wide group of abortion rights proponents and chronicles the evolution of abortion.

Periodicals

Amy Bach, "No Choice for Teens," *The Nation*, October 11, 1999.

Christopher Daly, "Gunman Kills 2, Wounds 5 in Attack on Abortion Clinics," *Washington Post*, December 31, 1994.

Jennifer Doran, "Constitutional Law: Three Bans on Partial-Birth Abortions Deemed Unconstitutional," *American Journal of Law and Medicine*, Winter 1999.

Winston Fritsch, "The Abortion Wars Come Home," *Newsweek*, November 9, 1998.

Julie Hirschfeld, "House-Passed Ban on Evasion of Parental Notification Laws Faces Senate Procedural Hurdles," *CQ Weekly*, July 3, 1999.

Carole Joffee, "Reactions to Medical Abortions Among Providers of Surgical Abortion—An Early Snapshot, Parts 1 and 2," *Family Planning Perspectives: The Alan Guttmacher Institute Newsletter*, January-February 1999.

Mark Kaufman, "Abortion Drug Proposal Criticized," *Washington Post*, June 7, 2000, p. A01.

National Abortion Federation, "What is Medical Abortion?" (fact sheet), January 2000.

National Abortion Federation, "What is Surgical Abortion?" (fact sheet), January 2000.

Quoted in Joni Scott, "From Hate Rhetoric to Hate Crime: A Link Acknowledged Too Late," *The Humanist*, January-February 1999.

Timothy J. Vinciguerra, "Notes of a Foot Soldier," *Albany Law Review*, Spring 1999.

Cases, Laws, and Hearings

Carhart v Stenberg, 92 F3d 1142 (8th Cir. 1999), No. 99-830.

The Hope Clinic et al. v James E. Ryan, Attorney General of Illinois, et al., No. 98-1726 (7th Cir., October 26, 1999).

House Committee on the Judiciary, Subcommittee on the Constitution, *The Partial-Birth Abortion Ban Act: Hearings on H.R. 1833*, 105th Cong., 1st sess., 1996.

Senate Committee on the Judiciary, *The Partial-Birth Abortion Act: Hearings on H.R. 1833*, 104th Cong., 1st sess., 1995.

Planned Parenthood of Central Missouri v Danforth, 428 US 52 (1976).

Internet Sources

"The Child Custody Protection Act and the Inadequacy of Judicial Bypass Procedures," September 1998. www.naral.org/publications/facts/bypass_97.html.

Frederick Clarkson, "Anti-abortion Violence: Two Decades of Arson, Bombs, and Murder," *Southern Poverty Law Center Intelligence Report*, Summer 1998. www.splcenter.org/intelligenceproject/ip4g2.html.

"Court Nixes Nebraska Abortion Law," *New York Times*, June 28, 2000. www.nytimes.com/aponline/w/PA-Scouts-Abortion.html.

Family Research Council, "Bauer Denounces Clinic Bombing," January 29, 1998. www.frc.org/press/012998a.html.

T. Trent Gegax and Lynette Clemetson, "The Abortion Wars Come Home," *Newsweek*, November 9, 1998. dailydavos. com/nw-srv/issue/19_98b/printed/int/us/na0119_l.htm.

Diane Gianelli, "Abortion Rights Leader Urges End to 'Half-Truths,'" *AMNews*, March 3, 1997. www.ama-assn.org/sci-pubs/amnews/pick_97/spec0303.htm#top.

"Mifepristone: FDA Proposes 'Tight' Restrictions for Abortifacient," *Kaiser Daily Reproductive Health Report*, June 7, 2000. http://report.kff.org/archive/repro/2000/06/kr000607.1.htm.

National Abortion Federation, "Testimony of Emily Lyons Before the House Judiciary Committee on Crime," July 17, 1998. www.prochoice.org/violence/emily_lyons.htm.

———, "Testimony of Marne Greening Before the Subcommittee on Crime and Criminal Justice," May 6, 1992. www.prochoice.org/violence/greening.htm.

Mark Pelavin, *Religious Action Center Newsletter*, January 29, 1998. www.rj.org/rac/news/012998.html.

Margaret Talbot, "The Little White Bombshell," *New York Times Magazine*, July 11, 1999. www.nytimes.com/library/magazine/home/19990711mag-abortion-pill-html.

Index

Picture Credits

Cover photo: Corbis/Stephanie Maze
AP/WideWorld/Troy Maben, 41
AP/WideWorld/Mauviniere, 66
AP/WideWorld/Toby Talbot, 56
FPG/Dick Luria, 46
FPG/Telegraph Colour Library, 42
Impact Visuals/Donna Binder, 29
Impact Visuals/J. K. Condyles, 73
Impact Visuals/Jerome Friar, 9
Impact Visuals/Ansell Horn, 50
Impact Visuals/Marilyn Humphries, 21, 36, 60
Impact Visuals/Michael J. Keating, 75
Impact Visuals/Kenneth Martin, 76
Impact Visuals/Meryl Levine, 22
Impact Visuals/David Rae Morris, 31
Impact Visuals/Shia Photo, 30
Impact Visuals/Kuni Takahashi, 7
Photodisc, 14
Photo Researchers/Spencer Grant, 33
Photo Researchers/David R. Grossman, 63
Photo Reseachers/Petit Format/Nestle/Science Source, 11, 58
Photo Researchers/Erika Stone, 54
Sipa Press/Nina Berman, 13, 17, 69
Sipa Press/Chavez, 34
Sipa Press/Jose Nieves, 27

About the Author

Award-winning children's magazine editor and writer Allison Lassieur has published more than two dozen books about history, world cultures, current events, science, and health. She has written for magazines such as *National Geographic World, Highlights for Children, Scholastic News*, and *Disney Adventures*, and also writes puzzle books and computer game materials. In addition to writing, Ms. Lassieur studies medieval history. She lives and works in Easton, Pennsylvania.